MW00477113

"Clayton Moore provides a highly engaging and personal account of his experiences as the first African-American police officer in a small town with big city problems. His own fight for justice reveals a great deal about race relations in the United States, making it an essential book in these turbulent times."

—Robert Alexander, PhD., Director, Institute for Civics and Public Policy at Ohio Northern University; CNN contributor

"Former Sgt. Moore's book was compelling, insightful, heart-rending, and thought provoking all at the same time. Recommended reading for anyone analyzing America's interaction with the police of today."

—Attorney and former Akron Municipal Court Chief Civil Magistrate and appointed Judge, Orlando J. Williams

"Clayton Moore's *Good Cop, Black Cop* is a real-life story riddled with lies, conspiracy, bigotry, implicit biases, a fall from grace, evidence, case files, suggestions, solutions, strength, perseverance, faith, and fortitude. It's all in there! No matter your race, background, or preference, at the end you're left staring at the person in the mirror asking yourself some very important life questions."

—Angel A. D. Tucker, Officer, Oregon, Ohio Police Department, Certified Instructor in the Midwest for Tactical Communication; Certified Instructor: Blue Coverage, Below 100, and Bridges Out of Poverty

"A captivating story of a well-known, Black police offi-cer serving in a small, Caucasian community whose life becomes entangled with hidden agendas to cause his destruction. This book parallels the current social injus-tices in our nation."

—Tasha Y. Jenkins, M.D.

"I have witnessed and experienced many things as a citizen of the world, but I have never understood the depth and range of human vision surrounded by sheer pain until reading Good Cop, Black Cop. Simply brilliant and rele-vant to this moment in history! A must-read."

—Lord Sam Orum, CEO & Founder of
1Voice Worldwide

"Clayton Moore's reality is powerful, eye opening, and disappointing at the same time as he takes readers through his life as a small-town sports hero to a Black man looked down upon and lies told about him. A Good Cop he definitely was, but being a Black Cop put him in a trap that almost ruined his life. Everyone needs to read this TRUTH!"

—Chetaun Smith, owner of Vision 20/20 Realtors
LLC and Vision 20/20 Consulting LLC,
author of *You've Got the Job, Now What?*

Good Cop, Black Cop: Guilty Until Proven Innocent

A Memoir

Clayton Moore

Copyright © 2021 by CLAYTON MOORE
All rights reserved.

No part of this publication may be reproduced, stored in a retrieval
system, or transmitted in any form or by any means, electronic,
mechanical, scanning, recording, photocopying, or otherwise,
without the prior written permission of the author.

Limit of Liability/Disclaimer of Warranty: This publication
is designed to provide accurate and authoritative information
in regard to the subject matter covered. It is sold with the
understanding that neither the author nor the publisher is engaged
in rendering legal, investment, accounting or other professional
services. While the publisher and author have used their best efforts
in preparing this book, they make no representations or warranties
with respect to the accuracy or completeness of the contents of
this book and specifically disclaim any implied warranties of
merchantability or fitness for a particular purpose. No warranty
may be created or extended by sales representatives or written sales
materials. The advice and strategies contained herein may not be
suitable for your situation. You should consult with a professional
when appropriate. Neither the publisher nor the author shall be
liable for any loss of profit or any other commercial damages,
including but not limited to special, incidental, consequential,
personal, or other damages.

GOOD COP, BLACK COP
Guilty Until Proven Innocent: A Memoir
By CLAYTON MOORE
1. BIO027000 2. BIO002010 3. POL014000
ISBN: 978-1-949642-57-5
EBOOK: 978-1-949642-58-2

Cover design by LEWIS AGRELL

Printed in the United States of America

Authority Publishing
11230 Gold Express Dr. #310-413
Gold River, CA 95670
800-877-1097
www.AuthorityPublishing.com

CONTENTS

AUTHOR'S NOTE

This is a work of nonfiction. My personal experience and the events associated all happened and are outlined herein according to my best recollection and the documents available. The conversations included are recreated to the best of my recollection, and while not word-for-word, they reflect the tone and content of the original conversation. Some names and identifying details have been changed to protect people's privacy and confidential information.

FOREWORD

The first time I ever worked out with Clayton was as a punishment. My sister, Meghan, had a bunch of kids over in the middle of the night one night. When my mom woke at 2:00 a.m., the kids scattered and hid. They weren't my friends, but I was awake, so I hid too. When my mom found us, she was not happy. Meghan got grounded, but our mom made me go to conditioning training with my older brother the next day.

I cried all day leading up to the conditioning session with Coach Clayton. I pleaded with my mom, "His are the hardest drills…" She wasn't hearing it. My argument that those kids weren't even my friends didn't move her. She reminded me of the extent of my punishment: that I had to do the entire set of drills like everybody else. Later that afternoon, I walked my middle schooler self onto the field full of high schoolers.

As I'd imagined, it was horrible. But halfway through, I thought, *You know what, it is what it is. I'm just as athletic as these high schoolers anyway, so I might as well make the most of it.* When I got to high school, Clayton became my football coach and after that my stepdad. A few years ago, Clayton told my mom that ever since that day on the football field he knew I was going to be something special because I sucked it up and went to work.

I attribute part of my success to Clayton's belief in me. When he gets something in his head, he's the most passionate person ever. He just won't quit. He has a vision, and he sees it through.

This book reflects his vision. Yes, it's about how he was wrongly accused of misconduct and what he went through in an attempt to clear his name, but it's more than that. It's about identity. It's about community.

As I was considering what to say in this foreword, I was asked how I identify myself—as a black man or in some other way. The conversation that followed started with the obvious lines of discussion. My initial answer was that I don't predominantly identify as black or white. I feel for both. I understand both. I can put myself in a white person's shoes and understand what she or he is talking about just like I can put myself in a black person's shoes and understand what he or she is talking about. As a biracial person, I honestly feel like I have the best of both worlds; I don't have to choose between identifying as black or white.

But as the conversation unfolded, I shared examples of Clayton's love of his hometown and the people in it: the fact that he recently painted his home workout room red and black, Fostoria high school's colors; how for as long as I can remember he's been involved with Big Brothers Big Sisters; and what being a Fostorian means to him. I realized that although Clayton is a black man, his identity doesn't come from that. His community and his place in it are where he gets his identity.

If you're nearly sixty years old and painting part of your house your high school colors, that's passion. That's passion for football. That's passion for where you live. When you grow up in a small town like we did, I think you tend to want to defend it, to do your part to make it better. That's how we all were growing up. We've always talked about giving back to Fostoria: *As soon as we get out of college, as soon as we get some money in our pocket, we want to give Fostoria a new football stadium. We want to give Fostoria a new downtown.* To this day, we still talk about stuff like that.

When I was in college, I got my first opportunity to make good on those dreams. I was fortunate. I got to go to college on a football scholarship. It was while I was there that I started the Imagine for Youth nonprofit. I wanted to give back and not just to kids in my hometown but kids around the nation. We started with sports equipment, and now we do football camps and give away backpacks and school supplies. Eventually we want to offer substantial academic scholarships to kids who otherwise wouldn't be able to go to college. My position as an NFL player has certainly helped attract supporters, but what I want is for the foundation to become its own thing, to be self-sustaining and not attached to my name. I want it to have its own identity because it's not about me. When my business professor challenged us to create an organization, I did what I'd always wanted to do. I guess you could say that I answered that call to action.

"Police officer" is an identity. "Serve and protect" is a calling.

We all have multiple identities, and we answer many calls. But I think the people who are the happiest and most effective are the ones who find their place in the world by finding where passion, identity, and calling intersect and then do everything in their power to defend it and create a safe haven for others.

Through his public service, perseverance, and this book, Clayton empowers and encourages people of all ethnicities, backgrounds, and beliefs to embrace what is (whether fair or unfair), overcome obstacles, and be forces of good.

Some of you may have been attracted to this book because you've experienced a wound similar to Clayton's. Some may have come for the opportunity to see life from a point of view that differs from your own. Others may know Clayton and want to get to know him better. Regardless of why you came to this book, I hope you'll leave as I did, more grounded in who you are and with a better sense of how important you are to the people in your community.

Micah Hyde
Starting defensive back for the National Football League's Buffalo Bills and Founder of Imagine for Youth

PROLOGUE

In August of 2008, the local paper published an article about me. It wasn't the first time, but this one was different. Previously, they'd been about my athletic performance and community service. This time it was an article titled, "Officer's personnel file loaded with allegations," and it listed the sixteen reasons cited for my termination from the Fostoria Police Department.[1]

It took me a long time to even be able to say the word "fired." "Let go," "laid off," "terminated." I used any word or phrase other than "fired." It was an incredibly painful time in my life, but all the things that happened during and after that time made me feel like God was telling me, "I'm taking care of you. Yeah, I know they pushed you out, but you know what, there are better things for you on the horizon, and you're gonna see that." And why would I have felt any other way about it? Whatever had been done to me or by me in my life that was bad, God has always turned around and made good. So, yes, I was fired, but that's not the end of the story.

When people hear my story, they often say, "You should write a book!" I thought about it for a long time but resisted for various reasons. After the 2016 election and with all the controversy over the Black Lives Matter movement, I couldn't resist writing this. That desire to put my thoughts to paper for others meant I'd have to overcome my biggest fear—the fear of letting people down, that I won't live up to what I want this to be.

I think a lot of you have a similar fear. Like me, I suspect that you aren't afraid to take that step of doing something you feel so strongly about, something that will expose you but might make a huge difference in someone's life or your community or state, or maybe even contribute to a shift in thinking on a nationwide level. None of us know how far our ideas will travel and how deep of an impression we might make. Like me, you probably want to make sure you're taking enough good steps to make a difference.

That's what this book is for me. It's the step I need to take. I can only hope and pray that it is enough and that I can make an even bigger difference by sharing it with you.

Good Cop, Black Cop offers a nuanced approach to the topic of what it means to be black in twenty-first century America, including my experiences growing up and joining the police force, learning the ropes and becoming established, then dealing with my downfall and fight to get my job back. It explores my contradictory thoughts and feelings about race and justice and one of the most polarizing social movements in modern history.

My hope is that by being as candid as possible in my not-yet-totally-consciously-evolved humanness (you know, the state we're all in whether we admit it or not), I can offer space for a conversation between all people: the secular and faithful, conservatives and progressives, cops and convicts.

Active duty or retired, being a police officer is an identity. We've taken an oath to serve and protect. This book is an extension of that mission. I hope it contributes to the conversation about racism and its human cost by offering a perspective that bridges the gap between officers and civilians, officers of color and white officers, conservatives and liberals, and every person who contributes to (consciously or unconsciously) or is affected by institutional racism. My mission is to create change somewhere, change that relieves pain, gives hope, and empowers readers regardless of their color to do *something*—to stand up, kneel down, or reach out in some way to people they may not have otherwise, and to view the world through a lens that acknowledges but does not judge based on the color of a person's skin.

CHAPTER 1

I AIN'T TRYING TO BE
NO COP

*M*y older brother, Larry, was a super athlete. I mean he was a stud. I should say that he could have been a stud, but, like a lot of kids in the neighborhood, he chose to smoke a lot of weed and go off and do his own thing.

Growing up, I always went to the grocery store with my mom because I wanted to pick out the cereal. It wasn't about the cereal. It was all about the toy in the cereal box. I wanted the toy, and I wanted to pick what it would be. Going to the store with Mom was the only way to make sure I got what I wanted.

One Saturday morning when I was in the fourth or fifth grade, Mom stopped by the cab stand where my dad worked. We'd just been to the store, and I was sitting in the front seat holding the cereal box. We kids had figured out that the toy was always at the bottom, so we started opening the boxes from the bottom end instead of the top like you're supposed to. I was messing with the bottom box flap, but I was not so distracted as to miss the conversation happening just outside my window.

Dad looked at Mom and said, "So he never came home?"

"No," my mom said.

The cereal box suddenly became less interesting. I shifted my attention to my parents and remember the looks on their faces even now. "He" could only be one person.

"Okay," Dad said.

They said some other things and then we left. I fought back tears. I looked at my mom. She was fighting them back too.

"Mommy?"

"Yeah?"

"Did Larry run away from home?"

She looked at me and let out a little laugh. "Why you ask that? What is that from?"

Neither of us said anything for about ten seconds. I looked at her. She looked at me, and I said, "Did he?" I was like Tom Landry, stone-faced. "Did he?"

She didn't answer. She just started crying, and the hurt and the pain I saw in her face made me say to myself, *I'm going to do something to make you guys happy, put a smile on your faces.* That day I decided I didn't want to have anything to do with drugs or cigarettes or anything that would mess me up. It was a choice I made as a kid, and all it took was seeing the hurt on mom's face as she sat in the family car that day.

Larry came back but ended up quitting high school and joining the Army. I chose a different path, but that's not to say I didn't face some of the same challenges.

* * *

Like a lot of junior high kids in the mid-70s, my friends and I played sports and hung out around town. In the evenings after basketball practice, my friends and I would walk over to the Kroger that was near the school to get snacks. Don't ask me why, but it was always orange juice and doughnuts and chocolate milk, and we'd pass them around. We'd all pitch in for doughnuts and drink out of the same container. We didn't care. To us, it was like drinking from the same water bottle during practice. So, week after week, we passed everything around, and everyone ate and drank the same thing. One day, something else got passed around.

One evening, my partner Billy Lawson and I were standing around drinking juice and eating donuts with the other guys when someone passed us a joint. When it was our turn, we took it; we took a puff and everything. I knew this was going to become a thing, part of our after-practice ritual. I knew that if my parents knew what I was doing, they would kill me.

The next day when we walked to the Kroger, I turned to Billy and said, "Are you going to do that, man?"

"I don't know, are you?"

"No, I'm not," I said.

I could still see my mom and dad's faces on the day Larry ran away. I had no desire to do it. It wasn't just that I didn't *want* to; I was scared of the consequences. Even then, I think I had some sense about predictable outcomes.

Billy looked at the other guys, then back at me and said, "Me neither. I'm not going to do it."

It was that day that Billy became a brother to me, a real partner I can depend on. I was best man at his wedding, and he was best man at mine. To this day, we're close, and people seemed to understand that. They knew we didn't want to have anything to do with reefer or any other substance that we could get in trouble with. Our friends respected our decision, and nobody else ever forced it on us either. Being athletes helped because most people don't mess with the athletes. Athletes are role models, whether they're ten or forty.

Later, as a coach and police officer, I'd go to schools and talk to kids about drugs and peer pressure. Like the pushers and other people, the kids had some respect for me because when I was in high school, I went to state in wrestling and track. The high school had even retired my jersey. I'd also played college ball. I think in a lot of ways, small-town heroes are what all kids are really looking for, someone like them who when faced with a hard choice took the better road.

They look up to me. I'm Coach Moore, and I always say to them, "You know doing all those things, that ain't cool you guys. You know what cool is? Cool is being yourself. That's what cool is." I talk about the courage it took and told them that if people don't like you for who you are and you're trying to fit in being somebody you're not, then they're not going to like you for being someone you're not, either. And you're not going to like yourself. I tell them straight up that their decisions don't just affect them. They affect their families, their friends, and their team. I remind them that they're connected to so many things besides themselves and that they must think about that.

I remind them of the importance of friendship and hanging with people like Billy because whenever I'm confronted with a hard choice, I know I can go to him. I always think, *That's my partner right there.* Everybody needs someone like that in their life.

Learning that it's not always about us is a lesson that takes a few go-rounds before it really sinks in. In a round-about way, Larry gave me my first lesson on that when I saw how his actions affected my parents and our family. My dad was the one to give me the second lesson one summer when I was playing baseball.

* * *

For years, I had played second base, and I was a pretty good second baseman. I thought I was the best second baseman in the city.

But one day, my coach, Charlie Carpenter, a man who had a great reputation around town for working with kids, pulled me aside and told me he wanted me to catch, to be a catcher.

"I'm not a catcher," I said. "I don't play catch. I'm a second baseman."

He told me who he wanted to play second baseman and reiterated that he wanted me to take the catcher position. I was hurt. I thought that I was better than that other boy and thought, *Why are you putting me at catcher?*

"Forget this. I'm quitting," I said.

Not long after that, my dad pulled me aside and said, "Hey, look. Charlie tells me you want to quit."

"Daddy, he got me playing catcher. I play second base. I'm better than that boy at second base, and he knows it."

My dad just listened, let me talk, and then as he always did in his soft-spoken way said, "Did you ever think that maybe coach knows that?"

"What do you mean?"

"Well, he probably knows that you're a better second baseman. However, maybe you're the best one that can play catcher on his team, and he has nobody else to fill that position. So, he needs his best player to do that, and that's why he chose you."

I had to think about that for a minute. It still wasn't what I wanted to hear and rejected it somewhat, and then my dad said, "You know, you can quit, but let me tell you something. Once you quit one thing the first time, it'll be easier for you to quit over and over again. And once you develop the habit of quitting, you'll always be a quitter."

I thought about other kids I knew. It was obvious to me even then that he was right. Quitters never do anything worth thinking about or admiring and always have some excuse that puts the blame on other people. I didn't want to be a quitter, and sports were my life. So I played catcher.

* * *

I don't know of any kid who plays a sport who doesn't dream of being a professional athlete, whether they're any good or not. I always wanted to be a professional athlete. I just love the game, to play. And I really loved playing the game of football.

No one even had to encourage me to play sports. I grew up in a neighborhood where the boys played sports. That's just what we did. But with everything happening with my brother, playing sports was a way for me to do something to make my parents proud, to give them their moment. Even as a high school and college athlete, I'd tell my younger brother, "Listen. It's not about us. It's not about us at all; it's not *our* moment. This is Mommy and Daddy's moment. Let them enjoy it even if sometimes they get on your nerves. Let them be proud parents because they deserve that." Anytime any of us kids have been in the spotlight, whether it was being in the paper or on television, my parents have always been proud of us and encouraged us.

"Mommy, what does this mean?" I handed my mom that day's paper. It was sometime in my freshman year of high school, and a local sports reporter had written an article about me titled something like "The Lone Ranger Strikes Again."

"Yeah, Clayton Moore. He was the actor who played the Lone Ranger. You were named after him."

That was the first time I remember hearing that, but after that, it came up a lot. From then on, when someone would say something about an article in the sports section that mentioned me, I'd say, "Yeah, I know. Lone Ranger."

I wasn't a lone ranger, though. At least I didn't feel like it at the time. I've always been a team player. The Lone Ranger moniker only got attached to me because of my name and how catchy it sounded. But it carried over when I became an officer. In that case, I could see similarities. At that point, it had nothing to do with my career or being an individual or a lone star. It was just that I carried a gun and a badge, and the Lone Ranger did the same.

My mother gave me my name. I think I got my athletic ability from her too. Not that she's much into sports, but she's played on a bowling league for about as long as I remember. She roller skates and does all kinds of things. She can draw anything and would even help me with school projects when I needed something drawn. She plays piano for her church and for her choir. She's always out doing things. She's the competitive one. If somebody does something, she's like, "Well, let me try this. Let me see what I can do." I like to think that I got my fun-loving nature and athletic ability from my mom.

But I got my tenacity and strategic thinking from my father. He taught me how to look for all the possible scenarios, recognize what's coming, and stay a few moves ahead. My tenacity and athletic skills blossomed early. The foresight and strategic part came a little later.

* * *

In the summer of my senior year at University of Toledo, I heard the words no up-and-comer wants to hear: "Clayton, I'm pregnant."

I was a good football player coming off a shoulder injury, and I desperately wanted to play in the NFL. I was a four-year starting linebacker at UT from 1981-84, the third leading all-time tackler with 414 stops, and I had 122 tackles in 1983 and 154 in 1984, both season highs.[1] I was getting ready for graduation and had the opportunity to try out for some professional teams. It was in the middle of football camp, right in the middle of doubles—two-a-day practice sessions—that I got the call from my girlfriend, Denise.

Right there during camp, I just lay in my bed and started crying. I felt like everything was gone, and I had to tell our parents. My parents respected me. Her parents respected me, and I respected them. In some ways that helped. In other ways, it made delivering the news more difficult. Years later, I'd find myself sitting in front of parents again delivering a different kind of difficult news.

"You need to get married," my mom said. "You're about to have a baby. You need to be married."

The knot in the pit of my stomach tightened even more. Again, I felt like all my dreams were totally gone.

It was different with Denise's dad.

"Clayton, if getting married isn't what you wanna do, then I don't want you to marry my daughter." Denise's dad has always treated me like a son. Up until his death less than a year ago as of this writing, he loved me unconditionally. "Son, don't do it if it's not what you want."

I couldn't hear him. The words were clear, but the meaning wasn't. The predictable outcome wasn't something I could see or was even looking for. I was too ashamed, and I wanted to right my wrong. Not just with Denise's parents but with mine too.

For the next week, I was sick. I was out of practice for several days throwing up. I was going through it. It had nothing to do with any physical ailment; it was the manifestation of my emotional state. I was hurt, and I didn't know how to deal with it. I couldn't lash out, so I turned my pain and anger inward.

I went back to practice. Playing through the pain helped. Burning energy through physical motion helped me focus and purge. I was fine after that. Denise and I made plans to get married during our break.

Between the last game of the season and the bowl game in December, we got married. Instead of staying on campus, Denise wanted me to move into her parents' home where she'd been living.

"We're married, Clayton. You should be here," she said.

"Yeah, but how am I gonna workout? I need to be here and get focused and work out with the guys and the coaches, and I can't be doing this driving back and forth." I saw my dream in front of me, but this situation forced me to do an about-face. It was like trying to run while carrying the weight of two other people on my shoulders, but it wasn't like they'd just jumped on me. I'd picked them up, by my actions.

I ended up moving off campus and in with her parents.

Just as I feared, I couldn't work out the way I wanted to. I couldn't get in the shape I wanted. I went to a couple of camps hoping to be scouted by the pros, but I didn't perform well. I was frustrated. Real frustrated. I put the blame on everybody but the person I saw in the mirror. I never came out and said it to anybody, but I saw Denise as the reason my dreams weren't coming true. In my eyes, she was a dream snatcher. Not my daughter, not me, her.

Denise and I had met when she was in junior high and I was in high school. Our moms bowled together and were in the same gospel singing group. Denise's mom was my youth group director in an NAACP youth group where I was president. Denise and I both went to one of their conferences in St. Louis, Missouri. She was a few years younger than me, but we became friends.

We'd ride our bikes around town together, and every now and then, we'd play a little tennis. She was just a little over 5 feet tall and only about 120 pounds at the time, and I was much bigger. I'm sure we made an odd couple, but we were just friends back then. It wasn't until college that we started dating.

When she graduated from high school in 1983, she went to Bowling Green State University, Toledo's rival.

She and I bumped into each other again when we'd each taken trips back home. We started hanging out again and not long after started dating. We'd always gotten along well and our families went way back.

After getting her pregnant, I decided to try to appease her, to make her happy. I felt like I owed her that. I felt like it was the least I could do. It wasn't about me. Every decision after that was about trying to make amends for what I felt like I'd done wrong. I lost myself. My identity was gone. If I could do it all over, I would have said, "You know what, we're both gonna raise this child. If we have to raise it separately that's fine, but I'm gonna stay focused. I'm gonna stay on track." I would have stayed on campus. I would have stayed in my apartment. I just would have worked out harder. I would have made it my purpose to make it. I would have worked hard for myself, for my dream, and I would have tried to use my success to appease her and the families—her family, my family, and all the people who looked down on me. If I could do it all over again, I would keep my eyes on my prize, my dreams, and let everyone else make the decisions they needed to make for themselves.

But that's not what happened. I let shame guide my actions. I let a bad decision define me in the moment, and, in my search for redemption, I did what was wrong for me. At least I knew that my parents were proud of my choice.

* * *

I was the first sibling to graduate from college. My parents wanted me to go to college and graduate, but it wasn't something they forced me to do. I'd always known I was going to do it, and in 1985, I graduated from the University of Toledo with a bachelor's in communication and a minor in broadcasting. I'd known what I wanted to study since the third grade.

In third grade, I was crazy about only two people: Muhammad Ali and Howard Cosell. I idolized Ali because of everything he'd gone through, and I loved how he was always rhyming and talking crap. That intrigued me. I liked that. I used to go around the house bothering my sisters. They'd say things like, "You always trying to rhyme. Quit always trying to rhyme everything, emulating Muhammad Ali!"

I had also started watching *Monday Night Football*. It got to the point where I wasn't even watching the game, I was just listening to Howard Cosell and his use of vocabulary. He used words that captured my attention and made everything he said vivid and compelling. I thought, *I wanna do what he does*. Before that, I'd wanted to be an attorney. I was a little kid thinking about going to school and becoming a lawyer. But, after watching *Monday Night Football* and being mesmerized by Howard Cosell and his words, I decided I wanted to go into broadcasting, into communications. Later, I found out that Howard Cosell had been an attorney.

He was everything I wanted to be except for being a professional football player himself. Having not done well at the camps I'd attended and with a baby on the way, I put my dreams and diploma on the shelf and got a part-time job working at the Meijer department store in Findlay, Ohio. It was money. It wasn't real money, but it was money. At that point, every decision I made was based on financially supporting my family. At least I worked in the toy and sporting goods section where I could mess around with other employees and throw a football every now and then. I was a terror. Thankfully, my former art teacher had been working there and was the one who hired me. I think she liked and took pity on me, so I never got into any trouble that threatened my job there.

Later that summer after I'd graduated from college and while working at Meijer, my high school coach, Richard Kidwell, offered me a coaching job. I jumped at the opportunity. It was a seasonal contract, but it meant six paychecks throughout the coaching season. It didn't pay the bills, but it helped a little bit. Unfortunately, that wasn't sustainable, and I did have the foresight to see that.

One afternoon my mother said, "Hey, they're giving a test for a police officer." She said it all casual, didn't just blurt it out. She had stopped over and made small talk for a while, but I could tell she had an agenda. And there it was.

"I don't care if they're giving a test. I ain't trying to be no cop!"

My mother didn't respond, just stood there cool as can be. I said, "That don't faze me. What's that got to do with me?"

In spite of the pulled muscles and not doing well at that summer's football camps and being newly married and having a new baby, I was still working out and thinking I had a shot at the pros.

I looked at her and said, "Mommy, I'm gonna be fine."

"Have you heard anything back from any of those places you put an application in?"

I hadn't and she knew it.

When I left school, I hadn't even used the college services or asked my advisors about how to get a broadcasting internship or anything else. I didn't engage in any of that. I just left and went out on my own. I was still ashamed. I was hurt. I was angry. I didn't show it. I wasn't rude or mean to people. I was mad at myself more than anything and sabotaged myself rather than getting over my pride and asking for help.

"Well, they're giving a test at the police department, at the city building for police officers." It wasn't the kind of statement that required me to answer.

With little else going for me, I figured I could at least go for higher pay and benefits. There was nothing about being a police officer that was attractive to me, other than it being a way to make a decent living while I waited for a pro team to pick me up.

CHAPTER 2

MAKING HISTORY

*I*n the fall of 1985, I pulled into the parking lot of Fostoria High School to take the Civil Service exam. The cafeteria was full of other residents hoping to get the single opening on the police force. The population of Fostoria was at that time between 16,000 and 17,000 people. They were all there for the same reasons I was—decent pay and benefits.

When I walked into the room, I felt like a loser. In my mind, the only reason I was there was because I was a loser. About halfway through the nearly two-hour written exam, I looked up and scanned around the cafeteria. I looked at everybody. I did it twice and thought, *Wow, all these people in here, and they're only gonna hire one person. That's crazy.*

Ten minutes later, I looked around at the crowd of people and thought, *Shoot, it's gonna be me!*

There was no arrogance, no cockiness. I just felt that it was going to be me. I was a college graduate. I was athletic. I am a minority. I thought that I checked all the boxes, and it wasn't because of affirmative action. That's not the way that works. Affirmative action wasn't established to give preferential opportunity to people of color and other minority groups; it was to give *equal* opportunity.[1] I knew I was the most qualified, and I happened to be black. I knew there had not been a single other African American on the police force in Fostoria, and I somehow knew that it was time. My time.

I thought, *There's nothing anyone in this room can do that I can't do and maybe do it even better.* Like I said, my mother and I are a lot alike.

I passed the written test without any problem and got invited to move on to the physical assessment, an all-day affair in late September or early October. With only 7% body fat, I was in the best shape of my life. I knew I had this.

Part of the agility test was to run, jump, and pull dummies. It wasn't that much different than the NFL combine. I had no problems. I was used to working out in that kind of weather. A lot of the other candidates were not, and by the end of the day when the weather was hotter, tempers flared and focus waned. Not mine. I was cool, Clayton cool.

One of the last tests of the day was a timed challenge. We were given three or four minutes to change a tire on a police vehicle. Several teams had already failed the exercise. Mine was the last to go.

When the signal sounded, I grabbed the jack to raise the vehicle but couldn't get it to work. It wouldn't raise. It was stuck. I couldn't get the tire off, and time expired. We failed. I failed.

But some sharp-eyed test administrator noticed that due to the heavy use throughout the day, the threads on the jack had been stripped. All the groups that had flunked were allowed to retake the test because of the malfunction in the equipment.

I got my second chance. This time, I passed.

Having passed the general aptitude and physical tests, I moved on to the psych test.

* * *

"You're awfully enthusiastic for someone about to take a polygraph," the polygraph administrator said as he finished wiring me up.

I couldn't stop grinning. All the police procedural television and movie scenes played through my mind. It was real and surreal. For some dumb reason, I thought this was pretty cool.

"You got any questions?" he said. He had that experienced cop look and his facial expression hinted at him having more questions about me than he was going to ask.

"No, I'm good, man. Let's do this."

The polygraph went well, I thought. But what did I know? I'd only ever seen this play out on screen. The guy did stop to ask me, "Why are you smiling? Something funny?"

"Nope. I'm just having fun," I told him. After a thorough round of questioning, he set his pencil down and leaned back in the squeaky, metal, taxpayer-paid-for chair.

"Alright, Mr. Moore, you passed. We're done, but are you sure you don't have no questions?"

"Yeah, I got one question."

"Okay. What is it?"

"You know in watching all these movies on television you always see when people try to beat the polygraph machine, you know? I've always thought I could beat a polygraph machine."

"You wanna try?"

"Yeah. Yeah. I wanna try."

I guess that old guy was hard up for entertainment because he started the whole thing over again. I tried but couldn't beat the machine.

"Thank you," I said as he reached to unhook me. "I just always wanted to do that. That was fun."

"I gotta say, you're about the happiest guy I've ever seen do this."

The next step was the background check. Maybe. They were only going to do that for the candidates with the highest raw scores. Extra points were given to candidates who'd served in the military, but college points weren't a thing. I'd just have to wait and see.

Winters in Fostoria are cold and snowy. Keeping the driveway cleared off was somewhat of a full-time job. One afternoon while I was out shoveling snow, Denise poked her head out the door.

"Clayton, you have a phone call," she yelled.

I had snot running down my nose, and my fingers were about frozen.

"Who is it? What do they want?" I yelled back.

"It's the Mayor. They want to offer you the job."

I looked around and down at my shovel. "Tell them to call back. I gotta finish my driveway."

Looking back on it now, I can't help but laugh. I can't believe I said that. All I was thinking was, *I'm not coming back in to come back outside to do this. I'm finishing now. When I get done, I'll call you.*

When I was done and my hands warmed back up, I dialed the phone.

"Hello, Mr. Moore," said the inscrutable voice on the other end of the line. "We'd like for you to come in and sit down for a talk."

Downtown, after an exchange of pleasantries, the real interview began.

Mayor Beier kicked things off. "As I'm sure you gathered, Mr. Moore, you were one of our top three highest scoring applicants who passed the background check. Number three, actually, but that doesn't matter because we're interviewing all of you and will hire the man best suited for the job."

"We understand that you still have ambitions to play professional football. If we were to hire you," Charles Macias, the Safety Service Director continued, "and you were later offered a place on a pro football team, what would you do? Would you leave the department to play football?"

Without hesitation, I said, "Heck yeah, in a heartbeat."

The men looked at each other and went pale. I didn't try to close the awkward gap because that's where my heart was. Yes, I would leave because that was my dream. I couldn't say "No, I wouldn't do that." They would know I was lying. What kind of character would they perceive in me if I tried to hide the truth?

They must have appreciated my honesty, because next thing I heard from Macias was, "Well, Clayton, we'd like to offer you the position."

I accepted, and we all shook hands.

It turned out that the two guys ahead of me beat me by 1.5 and .5 points thanks to their extra-credit military points. All things being equal, I'd beaten them. But they weren't the players I wanted to beat. I wanted to be on a different team in a different field, but at least I knew I could support my new family.

On February 16, 1986, I officially became the first black police officer in Fostoria, Ohio.

CHAPTER 3

STIGMAS AND STREET CRED

*I*was lean and focused, still thinking I had a chance to play in the NFL, but it wasn't meant to be. However, I would find my way into the world of professional football years later. But before I could play a bigger game, I had to learn to serve. And, although I hadn't realized it at the time, my dad's example had prepared me for being a police officer and the father I wanted to be.

My dad was never an avid sports fan. He did like boxing and sometimes watched baseball on television or listened to it on the radio. That's why I'm a Yankees fan; that was the team he liked. We didn't get much time together because he was never home during the week. He ran Star Cab. He worked from early in the morning until late at night Monday through Saturday. Sundays he was off work, but Sundays were Sunday school in the morning and then church. When we'd come home from church, we kids would go out to play and do whatever unless we had to go back for an afternoon or evening program.

When I was really little, there was a picture of Martin Luther King, Jr. and the Kennedys in the back room of our house. I thought that picture of King was a picture of my dad. When I got older, I realized that it was Martin Luther King, Jr., but to me, my dad resembled MLK and had a spirit to match.

Daddy was a deacon in our church. We were brought up in the church and didn't have an option about whether to attend. If it was Sunday, our family was in church. We were in Sunday school. We were in service. If there was an evening program at church, we were there with butts in pews. Other than Sundays, I didn't get to see Dad much.

Even when I was in high school, my dad didn't watch me play a lot of games because he was the only cab driver in Fostoria for over thirty years. Everybody knew him. He was always doing things for other people. When he passed away, there were people who still owed him money. If someone couldn't pay, he'd say, "Okay if you don't have the money, I'm going to still take you where you need to go. Get to me later." That's just who he was.

My dad was a giver, but he missed most of my sporting events because he was doing for other people. That bothered me when I was young, but it didn't bother me as I got older because I knew that he was going to be at one of my games every year, the Parents' Night game, because he had to be there. Because I knew he would see me play that one time a year, I always wanted that game to be my best game. It was hard, but that's just the way it was.

When I got hired on at the police department and was still working several jobs, I thought, *Wow, I feel like I'm like my dad. I'm working this job, working a second job just providing for the family.* At that moment, I got it. My dad was a provider. He sacrificed himself for his family. And that's who I was. I was him. His priority wasn't to each individual child but to the family. I wanted to be in a position where our finances in that household weren't going to stop me from being there for each of my kids.

The example my father set showed me the way, my way. It also showed me where I didn't want to go. I admired my dad, but I wanted to be more than just a provider.

* * *

As a new police officer, I had a lot of experiences where I saw people at their best and worst. I learned to keep one eye on who they were and what we agreed on, and the other eye on what was wrong and how to avoid their mistakes.

A few months after being hired, I was sent with some other officers to follow up on a complaint of cable theft. Back then it was a common occurrence for people to steal cable so they wouldn't have to pay for the services, something like logging in with a friend's Netflix password today. It wasn't that big of a deal, kind of funny in some ways—all that trouble to avoid a relatively small monthly fee. The thing was that we'd caught wind that someone at this address was doing something else, so the house had been under surveillance for a while. The cable theft warrant was probable cause, a way to get in the house to see what was really going on in there.

I walked up to the house with the lead officer. The occupant answered the officer's knock on the door, and the officer gave him a copy of the search warrant. There was nothing the dude could do. As we filed in, the occupant looked at me and said, "Hey, Clayton, how you doing?"

"What's up, Calvin?"

I was looking around and thinking, *Crap. This isn't good.*

My friend, who everyone in town knew, was a few years older than me. He was a friend I'd grown up and played baseball with. Instead of calling me Officer Moore or Mr.

Moore, he was calling me Clayton. It was awkward. He was growing and selling marijuana. It was there in plain view, and now we had to arrest him.

As a new recruit, I assisted in the arresting process. We gave him a copy of the warrant and charges.

"Okay," was all he said aloud. His look said, "Yeah, you got me." We arrested him without incident.

"Okay, Calvin, this way," I said, after we handcuffed him. We escorted him to the cruiser. I put him in and took him to the station.

Thankfully that represented the majority of complaints and arrests we handled. They were mostly noncombative daytime warrant situations because we take a lot of officers with us to deter resistance. Daytime knock warrants were far more likely to be met with compliance than no-knock nighttime warrants. Nighttime warrants were dramatic because we always took an entry team.

My friend's arrest may not have been dramatic, but it was traumatic in some ways. I was embarrassed. I was embarrassed for him because I'd seen what he was doing, things that he may have been trying to hide from his friends and family. Because I was in the position I was in, he couldn't hide from me. I felt ashamed and embarrassed for him because I had to see him in this moment. I didn't want him to think that I would go out and tell people, "You know Calvin? He sucks, and he's this, this, and that," because that's not who I am or what I do. I felt bad for him that he was probably going through all these thoughts not knowing what I was going to think of him—if I was going to tell anybody or what would happen.

If there's one thing I've learned as a cop it's that one bad act doesn't define a person. If there's a second thing I've learned, it's that most people are cool right up until the time you say, "You have the right to ..." and then things can get weird because at that point people know their liberty is about to be taken away from them. What was cool and kosher one minute can break loose and become all holy hell after that.

* * *

"We've got a 1091.A, guys," the voice on the police radio crackled one night not long after Calvin's arrest.

"We've got this one," said Officer Pfeiffer, my training officer, as he turned around and headed for the address where a drunk driver had run his car into a lady's porch.

When we arrived, the guy was still in his car. Other than a bloody nose, he was fine. As we helped him out of the vehicle, we talked to him. This was clearly a DUI situation.

At one point, Pfeiffer turned to me and whispered, "You watch. It's gonna happen ..."

"What's gonna happen?"

"Just watch," he said as we turned back to the inebriated driver, and he motioned me to assist.

"Hey, Mo, you good?" I asked. The other officer knew our suspect by his first name, too. Like I said, it was a small town. Tom ("Mo") was a city employee who used to cut the grass at the stadium. He knew our fathers. We knew him, he knew us, and everyone knew that old Mo was a drinker.

After making sure he was fine and exchanging niceties, Pfeiffer said, "Well Tom, okay, I gotta read you your rights. You have the right to remain—" As soon as he said that, Tom just fell out, just passed out like he didn't want to hear the rest. It was like if he didn't hear the words, he couldn't get arrested.

I wouldn't have believed it if I'd been told about it, but seeing it happen was comical.

One second our suspect was talking to us while patting his nose with a tissue to stop the trickle of blood. The next second, upon hearing those words, he went limp and hit the ground.

That little stunt may have bought him half a minute more of freedom, but it didn't get him out of anything. We charged him, cuffed him, and put him in the cruiser.

Some guys go limp, some cry, some snap and get violent, and others run.

* * *

Between 1986 and 1996, we had some wannabe gangsters that had come to Fostoria from Toledo. In the course of my duties, I'd often talk to these guys. They didn't worry too much about the Fostoria cops but always wanted to know when I'd be working.

"Ain't no sense in me running from you because you going to catch me, but you're the only one," one guy said to me one night.

After chasing down another guy at a different time, he looked at me and said, "It figures. Of all the people that had to get the call, of course it had to be you."

That was the word on the street: "Don't run from Clayton. He *will* catch you."

I'd developed somewhat of a brand on the streets and thought I was the coolest cop on the force. Those other cops looked like beat cops. I was what you might call "too Cool," with a capital C, but it didn't last.

In the spring and summer, we were assigned what we called "summer hats"—ball caps. The hat I was issued was the right size for my head, but too small for my hair. My afro made the hat too small, but that was fine by me. I wore my cap backwards and sported a pair of Cool-Moe-Dee sunglasses, baby blue shutter shades. At the time, there was nothing on the books about exactly how we were supposed to wear our uniform hats or what type of non-issue sunglasses we could wear, and I would never wear the mirrored aviators that seemed to be a symbol of white cops.

Adding insult to injury, I went and had my ear pierced.

My captain at the time did not know how to take me, talk to me, treat me, you name it. I used that and ran with it, until my captain became the chief.

At the time I was hired, other officers wore earrings. One wore a small diamond stud, but that wasn't my style. Mine had to dangle, a small cross earring with a quarter inch gold chain and definitely COOL. That was too much, and Chief Mason issued the first of many directives that later became known as "The Clayton Directives." Earrings were out and off, thanks to Clayton Moore.

People knew my family, knew me. They knew I was a good guy despite my desire to stand out and the fact that I raised my fair share of eyebrows. Most of my fellow police officers welcomed me with open arms, although it was a different story with some of my supervisors.

For the first couple years or so, I got the distinct feeling that I was being followed. I'd see other units pass me when I was on patrol. The officer driving the car showed a keen interest in everything I was doing by slowing down and rubber necking. When I pulled in and out of the station, there was often another officer pulling in and out with me. In a city like Toledo or Chicago with their large police forces that would make more sense, but not in Fostoria. There just weren't that many of us to go around. It was as if the people who'd hired me and were charged with training me didn't trust me.

"Moore. You're late," my shift supervisor said one morning as I rushed into the briefing room.

I *was* late. I'd overslept.

Later, he told me he was docking my pay due to my tardiness. I couldn't believe it. One time. I'd been late *one* time.

A few weeks before another officer had slept in and stumbled in late. I went to her and asked if her pay had been docked. It had not.

Considering how the community responded to me and that other officers were trusted to just do their jobs and given the benefit of the doubt when they screwed up, I interpreted my situation like any person of color would. *It's because I'm black.*

I went straight back to my supervisor.

"I don't mind being punished for things I do or don't do but not when other officers do the exact same things and nobody says boo to them. You treat me the same as you treat everyone else."

Most people in the department quickly learned that I wasn't the kind to put up with any foolishness. At the same time, they saw what type of person I was and am, that I love to have fun and that community is very important to me.

Even as a young officer, I got involved with Big Brothers Big Sisters and organized several charity events with competitions between our department and other departments in the area. We had basketball games, softball games, and every other game you can think of. I spearheaded many of those things. I had street cred, and after a rocky start, I developed professional credibility. I was seeing things from even more angles than I ever had before, even if I wasn't allowed to see them through a fly pair of shades.

I started to become aware of how race, upbringing, personality, and life experience shape the way we see the world and interact with the people in it. That's not to say that it was all unicorns, rainbows, and bliss after that.

Pat Brooks and another officer were in a squad room one day talking about minorities and dating and kids and everything in between. Pat was loud. Everything he said was thirty decibels higher than it needed to be. He didn't understand the meaning of the word "whisper." There were times I was two and three rooms over and could still hear Pat talk. I'd often think, *Would you just shut up?*

"I would never have a black person date none of my daughters," Pat said. Being in the Sergeant's room, I heard and never forgot.

Brooks was about six feet and 190 pounds and looked like Gomer Pyle with a Sergeant Carter haircut. He had been in the Navy. He never seemed to be able to shake that military hierarchy thing and always wanted to have power and be in control. He did not like following orders, which is kind of ironic that he was in the service. He had a problem with authority, but he also seemed to have a problem with minorities, whether they be women or ethnic groups. He was the type of individual who put off the vibe of thinking he was better than other people.

He didn't engender trust or loyalty. In general, we all knew he was good at taking tests—book smart—but thought he was dumber than a box of rocks. Pat Brooks was a puzzle though, because there were times when he'd be really nice and we'd all be laughing, and I'd think, *Okay, maybe he's not so bad…* There'd be other times though when he was just an ass.

Brooks was the type who would elevate himself by putting others down. I think he felt like he was doing the right thing, like he was justified in everything he was doing. Unfortunately, he wasn't involved in the community and didn't even live in Fostoria. If there was more to him, none of us got to experience it.

The one thing about Brooks that people should know is that he was not a liar. He just didn't always get the facts right. He'd see one thing and run with it instead of getting all the data together. There were times when I'd call him on his sloppy analysis. At more contrite times, he'd say, "Shoot, I guess I should've done a better job."

"Yeah, you should have," I'd say. But when he got tunnel vision, he'd go with it.

Early on in our professional relationship, I was the OIC—Officer in Charge—on a shift we were both working, when I had to reprimand him. He got suspended with pay for one day. Not a big deal in the scheme of things, but while Pat wasn't a liar, he was vindictive.

These interactions set the stage for some drama that would play out years later.

CHAPTER 4

THE BADGE DELIVERS BAD NEWS

*B*y early November in 1986, I'd learned a lot while on the job, and I'd settled into fatherhood and family life. Early on, Denise and I had decided that even though we had a large extended family, we'd always take care of our kids first when it came to buying Christmas gifts. In early November of 1986, we were out shopping for presents for my sister's daughter and son.

"Don't get them junk, Clayton," Glenda had said when I asked her what she wanted us to get the kids for Christmas. "Get them something educational."

I was so excited when we were driving home from the store.

"I wanna stop by Glenda's on the way home," I said to Denise.

"Clayton, it's late. Everybody's tired."

"I won't be long. I just wanna show her what we got."

I was persistent, so happy with what I'd been able to do for her and for my family. Soon after, I pulled up in front of where Glenda lived in a low-income housing complex.

"Wait here. I'll be right back. I'm just going to have her come out and look," I said. I swung out of the car and closed the door behind me, then bounded up to her door.

"Come out here. I want to show you what we got the kids," I said when Glenda answered the door.

Glenda came out to the car, and I popped the trunk.

She smiled and gave me a big hug and said in her big, lively voice, "Thank you!"

Going to see her that night, in spite of my wife's objections, was one of the best decisions of my life. The memory of her arms around my neck will live with me forever.

* * *

On Saturday November 15th, I'd just finished working the midnight shift and had gone home and collapsed into my bed. I was half asleep when I heard a knock at my door.

The knock of a police officer is distinct, quite different from that of a regular person. A police officer's knock is meant to get a resident's attention. It demands an answer. I reluctantly pulled myself from the haze of hypnagogia and shuffled to the door.

By the time I opened the door, the cruiser had just pulled out of my driveway and was heading away from my house. I turned to close the door and go back to bed, but the driver must've looked in the rearview mirror because I saw the cruiser stop and come back.

Detective Hutchins and Captain Wilson stepped out of the vehicle and walked into the house.

Joel Hutchins had been a detective for a while and was a man of common sense. He knows how to talk to people. Roger Wilson had been in the military and was easily distracted. He'd been a helicopter pilot and loved to talk about choppers.

On days he started talking to my fellow officers, I would be thinking, *We don't care about no doggone helicopters*, but he'd just keep going. And because we were talking to the captain, we had a plausible reason for why we couldn't go on the road. Captain Wilson didn't even need to have people around to listen to him.

We would sometimes see him in the camera feeds that were from around the police department. He'd be walking outside to smoke a cigarette, and he'd look up and start talking. "Who's he talking to?" I said to a fellow officer one time. We looked out and there were birds in the trees. "I don't know if he's talking to the birds or what," I said. Whoever he was talking to, I liked this brother. He's a nice guy, but he didn't have Joel Hutchins' situational awareness.

"Do you have a sister named Glenda?" Wilson asked.

"Yeah." I sat down.

"She's dead," he blurted out.

It sounded like he was throwing something at me. I reacted.

I stood, and I went to grab him. I was out of my mind for a moment. Joel got between us.

"Clayton, Clayton, listen, listen," he said.

If he hadn't stepped in, I may have choked the living daylights out of my captain.

"Sit down, Clayton," Hutchins said. I complied.

Glenda was my big sister and so proud of me. After I got hired and started working the midnight shift, I'd sometimes see her and her friends when I was on patrol. When we got fight and other complaints from the club section of town, I'd often drive through to answer them or to be a presence in the area. When Glenda and her friends were out at the clubs, she'd sometimes see me. She'd run over to my cruiser or wherever I was, put her arms around me, hug me, and tell everybody, "This is my baby brother, y'all." Even when I was in uniform, she had no problem with hugging me. I'd be there trying to handle situations, and she'd be trying to show me off with, "Y'all, this is my brother." She was just full of life and light. She was everything to me and could do anything.

Our mom had taught Glenda how to cook when Mom was put on afternoon shift at the General Electric in Tiffin, Ohio. My mom was working there the night Glenda died. Glenda was supposed to be there when I was sitting in my living room receiving the worst news any officer can give or receive.

Sitting there in the early hours of the morning so tired I could barely move, my mind was traveling through three planes of time: the past, the present, and the future.

Glenda was a year older than me, but we were tight. I remembered all the times she'd made amazing food for me, cleaned up the house, and was there for me when our mom and dad couldn't be.

She'd gotten pregnant right after she graduated from high school and moved out of my parents' house and into low-income housing. For a while, I thought of her as kind of the black sheep of the family. She graduated from high school but didn't go on to college. She took a different path. At the same time, she did her thing. She was respectful, a single parent living and making things happen, and she supported all of us in everything we did.

"Clayton, your sister's car was struck by a train as she tried to cross the tracks. The rail was down, but it looks like she tried to go around it and beat the train."

On her way to work. Probably running late.

I nodded. The first thing I could think about was not about what I was feeling. It was about my parents and how they were going to handle the news, how her kids, my niece and nephew, were going to take it.

"We're gonna need somebody to come up to the hospital and identify her. We've already sent someone to find your dad's cab, and we can come with you to your mom's house to tell her if you want us to."

"She's not there. She and my other sister, Ava, are at work. That's where Glenda worked too. They usually drove together."

"Alright. When your parents give us a positive—"

"No. They can't do it. There's no way I'd let them do that. I'll do it."

By that point, I think Detective Hutchins and Captain Wilson felt that was best as well. Half an hour later, I was standing in a cold room, looking down at my sister.

It was her. Someone had smoothed her hair off her face. I instinctually reached up and touched my own. Growing up, she'd spend hours braiding my hair during the football season. She'd braid my hair, and we'd talk and laugh.

She was my sister. She was my big sister. Was.

My dad wouldn't come into the room. My mother couldn't.

Years later, I'd cite the woman who would later become my second wife for driving around the safety barriers at another train crossing. "I wish I could give this to my sister instead of you right now," I said as I handed her the ticket. The driver looked up at me as she took it.

"My big sister was killed when she tried to beat the train because she was late for work. Nothing is so urgent it's worth dying for," I said and walked away, trying not to remember.

A few days after the accident, my dad and I were standing in the back yard of my parents' house. It was just the two of us. "How'd she look?" my dad asked.

Glenda never saw the Christmas that was just weeks away. Some people believe that God gives us signs. Sometimes we're intuitive and can connect with them, and sometimes we're not. I look back now and think, *Wow, this is what he was telling me on the night I just had to go show her the gifts we'd bought her children.* It was His gift to me, His child, to give me the memory of her face that night and the feeling of her arms wrapped around my neck.

My dad loved his girls. We were like the Brady Bunch, three girls and three boys in our family. My dad loved his boys, but he had a special affection for his daughters; he *loved* his girls.

"She looked okay, Daddy. You know, she's okay." That wasn't the truth, but I could never let them know what I had seen. That was my gift to him.

He never brought it up again, and I've never regretted lying to him.

On Christmas Day, my niece and nephew sat in the living room of my parents' home and unwrapped the educational toys we'd gotten them. I felt the warmth of my sister's arms around my neck and thought back to a Christmas past when, like Sundays, we were all together. I don't want to say that we struggled, but we didn't know what we didn't have. We didn't know because we were just living life in a way that was normal to us, and we were fine. We never went without things we needed.

We may not have had a lot, but we had each other. And we had socks.

My Christmas present from my sisters one year was a pair of socks. One sister wrapped up one of the socks; the other wrapped the other sock. When I got them together, I had a pair of socks. I thought that was great.

When my parents adopted Glenda's kids, I knew that even though money would still be tight, they'd always have what they needed, physically and emotionally. They were two and four at the time and spent a lot of time with my wife, daughter, and me. The girls were the same age and went to school together, and I talk to my niece regularly. When most people lose a loved one, there's no one to hold that place in their life. When I look at and listen to my niece, I see and hear her mother, my precious sister.

* * *

Years later, I stood on the doorstep of a couple who were good friends of my family. My parents knew them, and my brothers and sisters and I had gone to school with their kids. We'd all gone to the same church.

I felt a sharp pain as my knuckles struck the door. *Knock. Knock. Knock.*

It was nothing compared to the pain the people on the other side of the door were about to experience.

"Who's that?" Mrs. Smith asked from behind the door.

"This is Officer Moore. It's Clayton."

"Oh, Clayton, is everything okay?" she said as she opened the door and motioned me inside.

Everything was not okay. We'd received a call from the Toledo Police Department which is located about an hour north of us. A Fostoria man in his mid-thirties had died suddenly.

I stepped into the house. The house was very dark, like someone had used low-watt bulbs in all the fixtures. I saw a dim light in the kitchen down the hall beyond the front room where we were standing. To the right was a bedroom.

"Mrs. Smith, are you by yourself?"

"Yeah," she said and nodded, obviously concerned.

"You're the only one home? May I come in?"

"Yeah, come on in," she said. I stepped further into the house.

There was no one else there to comfort her, but the news wasn't going to change or get any easier to take. I had to do my job.

"Unfortunately, I have some bad news," I said. "We got a call from the Toledo hospital, and Mikey passed away a short while ago."

Without warning, she screamed.

Almost immediately after, I heard a man's voice coming from the bedroom.

Oh my God. There's somebody in the house! Adrenaline rushed into my bloodstream, quickening my heart rate and sharpening my senses.

I knew that they had weapons in the house. All I could think was *It's dark, a woman is screaming, and I'm right here, a male.* I thought, *I don't wanna have him come out shooting.* I'd have had to shoot and would likely kill him.

I remembered the light in the kitchen and quickly walked toward it. I stood right under it so he could see me, so he could see that the man who'd caused his loved one to scream was a police officer. It was just instinctive, the first thing that came to mind: *Be visible, let him know who you are.*

A man's form appeared from the gloom.

"Mo, Little Moore, is that you? Little Moore?"

"Mr. Smith, this is me. It's Clayton."

"What's going on?" he asked as both our bodies relaxed slightly. Mrs. Smith said nothing. She seemed to be in shock. I sat down at the kitchen table and asked them to sit too.

* * *

The adrenaline that had given me a shot of energy was beginning to wear off. As it receded, it felt like it was pulling the scab off the wound of my sister's death. All I wanted was to be as careful as I could and to protect them as much as possible. I leaned forward and in a soothing voice said, "I'm really sorry, Mr. and Mrs. Smith, but Mikey swallowed some drugs. They were in balloons, and one of the balloons opened up inside of him causing him to go into cardiac arrest."

They sat across from me and cried. There wasn't much to say. Words don't matter as much as just being there.

I stayed for a while, getting the sense from both of them that they were glad it was me that had come and told them, not anybody else. As I stood to leave, I said, "If there's anything you need, call me. I'm working for several more hours tonight. Whatever I can find out for you I'd be more than happy to."

They were appreciative and comforting each other and both hugged me as I left, which was a relief. Nevertheless, that had been one of the scariest moments of my life. I'd been by myself.

That night solidified the lesson to expect the unexpected because everybody reacts in different ways to different things. There's no wrong or right way necessarily; it's just the way people react to things. Be aware of that fact. Be mindful and respectful of it. Be prepared and be compassionate.

CHAPTER 5

A HOUSE DIVIDED

Thankfully, delivering death notices is a small part of a police officer's job. And although I did my fair share of giving tickets, arresting people, and testifying against them in trials, I balanced it by staying involved in the community and loving on my three little girls in ways my dad never got to.

Like my dad, I took my girls to Sunday school and church, although their mom only sometimes went with us. After work when I wasn't coaching, I hung out with them at the pool in our back yard. The girls loved being at home, and our house became a gathering place for all their friends and a place for me to be the dad and man I wanted to be.

When I wasn't around, the girls couldn't get in the pool because their mom wouldn't get in with them, and when I was around their mom didn't seem to care. What she did care about was me being around other women.

Me being a police officer seemed to highlight Denise's insecurities. Regardless of whether my interaction with females was in the line of duty, part of my community service, or church related, I had to be very careful about what I did and what I said. If I was around other women in public, I had to not appear to my wife as being overly friendly to other women. Who I am and what was in my heart didn't seem to matter. It was as if she didn't even know me or like me. She didn't want me; she wanted to possess me.

Although her reactions put a damper on things, I stayed involved in my passions—helping kids and finding any opportunity I could to be around new, fun, exciting people. Of course, I stayed close with my parents, siblings, nieces, and nephews too.

When my brother Damon, who's fourteen years younger than me, was in eighth grade, I started coaching his football team. One of the things I love about coaching youth is the opportunity to help them break what some call "generational curses." I've seen it. All police officers see it. The grandparents who've been in trouble all their life seem to raise kids who are in trouble and who have their own kids start acting out and flirting with a life "in the system."

Some cops get cynical. I never did because for me that would mean a change in how I treated people, and I never stopped treating people the way I wanted them to treat me despite what they were going through. I didn't make fun or light of what they were going through. I tried to lighten things up by saying things like, "Hey, it appears to be bad right now, we have to deal with it, but we'll get through this." I tried to take out the element of fear and hostility to deescalate situations. Maybe it's because I love people so much and try to see the best in any situation.

I did get a reality check though. The longer I was involved in law enforcement, the more I saw repeat offenders. Poverty and crime are passed down from generation to generation unless there's a disruption. I tried to be that positive interruption no matter who I was talking to or working with.

There were many occasions when I had exchanges with kids I was coaching or talking to.

They'd say, "You know my mom and dad? Yeah, my mom and dad know you. They said you arrested them."

"Yeah, I did, but you know what? Hopefully they were just going through a bad period, and I happened to be there."

I always hoped that people felt like I treated them right.

A majority of the time the kid or third party would say something like, "Yeah, they said you were real nice. They really like you."

"Well that's great," I'd respond. "Hopefully things worked out better after that." And then we'd get back on task.

* * *

Cops, like soldiers, tend to give each other nicknames. Early in my career, several supervisors told me that I was taking too long on some calls. They'd say, "I get what you're trying to do, but you can't save the world, Clayton." Other officers started calling me "Preacher" and sometimes "Minister." It took me a while to understand that and accept that I really couldn't save the world. But I did realize that I could change an individual. About those hardened and habitual petty criminals, I'd think, *Maybe they're like that because nobody's ever tried to talk to them. Maybe it's because nobody showed them that they care, or nobody said, 'Hey, there's another option.'*

There are so many people in Fostoria who still call me and come to me for help because I'm accessible. They know me; they know how involved I am.

At first, it was embarrassing to go on calls involving people I knew, but then I got it. Often, calls where an officer who didn't live in the community or who wasn't actively involved would get more heated. There was more confrontation. If I was there or showed up as backup, people sometimes said things to the first responder like, "Forget you. I don't want to talk to you. I'll talk to Clayton." It wasn't Sergeant Moore or Officer Moore; it was, "I'll talk to Clayton. I want Clayton to put the cuffs on me." It was extremely uncomfortable and not lost on me that more Caucasians than blacks asked to deal with me rather than the white officers present. Being dismissed by the people they were trying to deal with seemed to bother some of the officers, but things got done, and they got done in a calm, safe manner for all involved.

Being specifically selected by the people being arrested, irrespective of the ranking officer at the call, embarrassed me at first, but then I realized that that is one of the biggest compliments I could get. To know that I'm about to take away someone's liberty but to have me do it rather than someone else, is humbling.

I'm very proud of being called "preacher" or being seen as someone with a heart for people and someone who cares about what's going on inside of people, not just what's on the outside. That mentality allows me to look at things differently and as a police officer to see things from a perspective that's more grey than black-and-white.

* * *

When O.J. Simpson was arrested and tried for the murders of his ex-wife and her friend in the mid-90s, the consensus was that he was guilty as sin. This was especially true in law enforcement circles and the white community. Many in the black community truly felt he was innocent and being railroaded by the system in another example of unequal justice under the law. I believe there were many like myself who were asking more questions than just "Is he or isn't he guilty?" and looking past the facts of the case to the meaning.

As if prophetic, Johnnie Cochran's famous closing line, "If it doesn't fit, you must acquit!"[1] is almost as famous as the verdict: not guilty. Some people think O.J. got off because he didn't do it. Some people think O.J. got off because the prosecution and much of the expert testimony was horrible. I think O.J. got off because he had something that a lot of the minorities don't have: money.

O.J. Simpson had the resources to defend his case. Regardless of whether the outcome was right or wrong, he had the opportunity to hire a world-class defense team that could match the tools and resources of the prosecuting attorney's office.

In theory, the United States has a *blind* legal system where there is *justice for all*. In practice, proof "beyond a reasonable doubt" can easily be established when defendants do not have the resources to hire their own experts and attorneys who have the time to heavily invest in their clients' defense. Proverbs 18:17 says, "The first to plead his case seems right, until another comes and examines him."[2] O.J. Simpson had the resources to offer counterpoints and create reasonable doubt. The majority of African Americans, and many other minorities, don't have that luxury. There is ample evidence to show that this is a contributing factor to the majority of the people in jail being minorities, African Americans being at the top of that demographic. When the general population is predominantly white and the prison population predominantly black, it's not too far of a leap for many people—police officers included and perhaps especially—to think and even say out loud, "Of course he's guilty."

The procedural mistakes and unexplored avenues in O.J.'s case created reasonable doubt in my mind. But I must admit that the African American man in me celebrated, as I believe others did, the fact that there were black people coming up and in positions to defend themselves within the system should the need arise.

Despite the mishandling of evidence and inconsistencies, the consensus in the department was that O.J. Simpson was guilty. That was the only answer. Of course he did it. It was disheartening to me as a respected member of the community, a law enforcement officer, *and* a black man, that none of my fellow officers asked me what I thought about one of the most important cases of the decade. The conversation in the station centered on testimony that supported a guilty verdict, not in looking at every angle to test his guilt or innocence. Nobody seemed interested in walking a mile in O.J.'s shoes or understanding the motivations behind the black community's support of a man accused of such a heinous crime.

The color of my skin, my upbringing, and where I lived all helped me appreciate things and see perspectives that differed from my fellow officers. It allowed me to have empathy.

Empathy and involvement are wonderful in and of themselves, but police officers who embrace them are set up for failure in some ways. Seeing inequality and sometimes outright discrimination, and dealing with situations where people refuse to change no matter what you do, can cause burnout.

* * *

By the time Damon was in eighth grade, I was ready for a change. I've always wanted to live in a city or have access to a bigger city. At that time, I was becoming increasingly unhappy with the city of Fostoria and what it had to offer—what it *didn't* have to offer. The entrepreneurial, adventure seeking part of me wasn't being fed. While I loved the people of Fostoria, it didn't have the diversity I craved. It must have showed because on more than one occasion people commented on my big city mentality in a small town.

Playing in the NFL had long before dropped out of the realm of possibility for me, but being a police officer had still been second choice. I didn't know what I wanted to do, but big city was part of my first choice. I started putting out resumes to places far and wide. I stayed with my cousin in Atlanta and a friend, Steve "Stubby" Lehmann, in Chicago. I interviewed with IBM, Xerox, and other corporations in which I could use my communications degree. Some offered me jobs. As before, I had to make choices about my future based on the money attached. All were lower pay than I'd hoped for. All said it was because I didn't have any formal education in computer technology. They couldn't justify higher pay. If we moved, we'd go from two incomes to one at least for some amount of time. I couldn't risk lower pay.

I thought, *Okay, if I go back and get a computer degree maybe I can reapply and get a higher offer.* With that in mind, I enrolled in Stautzenberger College and signed up for a six-month program to obtain a certificate in microcomputers.

Damon had lost his eligibility to play football because of his poor grades, so I stepped in for my parents to make sure he did what he needed to finish his classwork and get his player status back. Part of that was dragging him with me to night classes so I could supervise him while he did his work. Not only did he get his grades up, he was on the honor roll for the following nine weeks.

It was a great time for me. I've always been good at math, so I excelled. One of my teachers asked if I would help some of the other students.

One evening I was helping one of the women in the class when she said, "You look nice today." That's all she said, "You look nice today." I was totally blown away, because somebody said something nice. After that, I started making sure I looked nice. Nothing extravagant or anything. I just wanted to look nice.

We started talking more and taking breaks together. She was not happy in her marriage. I'd never felt appreciated or respected in mine, and with what was going on in both our households our relationship was an outlet for both of us. I gravitated toward this healthier, friendlier environment. I had a choice. I made the wrong one.

After six months, I couldn't take the guilt. I had never done anything like this before. I wanted to do anything to make it right. I knew at the time that I was going to go through hell but thought, *If I have to go through it, I have to go through it. This is on me. I gotta be willing to take the punishment or whatever things I have to get through this.* It was such an egregious mistake, something that not only affected me and my family but the other woman's husband and kids too. The burden was more than I could carry.

One evening, I pulled Denise aside and said the words that never precede good news, "We need to talk."

I told her everything. She was irate, a predictable outcome that I couldn't avoid and had brought on myself. I sat there and took it. When she finally wound down, I said, "Please, Denise. I want to make this right, as much as I can. I want to go to counseling, do whatever it takes."

We did go to counseling. Denise was bitter. Who could blame her? But the road was harder than it needed to be. Everything went downhill from there.

Extramarital affairs happen in any work environment, be it the clergy or law enforcement, but the job certainly doesn't help, and police work seems to exacerbate the problem. The hours are long and shifts difficult to schedule family time around. The stress that officers are under and pressure to maintain confidentiality, especially in a small town, wear on a person's mind. During the first couple of years that I was in law enforcement, I was warned that there is a higher rate of infidelity among police officers. I was told that women would come on to me because a lot of people are attracted to the badge and uniform. I blew it off as a myth until I saw it firsthand.

Law enforcement officers are in a profession where we deliver aid. Help in the form of attention. Many people, for whatever reason, seek attention. If they're not happy in their own situation, they know they can call 911; we have to respond. Some people will do whatever they can to get attention and to give attention to the responder in the form of compliments and niceties. If the responder is in a bad situation or happens to like the attention, the situation is ripe for inappropriate behavior.

Despite Denise's fears, nobody ever came on to me in a sexual way, but as a police officer I did experience times when people expressed genuine gratitude and warmth as a reaction to something I did or said. If you aren't used to that, it's very powerful. You realize that just being nice to somebody is attractive, just like being told I looked nice flipped a switch in my head and pulled me into something I'd not sought out. It's easy to fall in love with that feeling or fall in *like* with it. It's kind of like a drug. You like that high. Infidelity is just one small step away, and for officers who don't get caught, the path of serial infidelity is easy to walk. People need love. They need companionship. Even as police officers we're people first.

I entered it fully aware of what I was doing, but it still came as a great shock to me. Under the right circumstances, all it took was for someone to appreciate me for my intellect and appearance, to say that they noticed me. In the end it was a lesson and regret I'll carry to the day I die. On the upside, it was one more experience that helps me see the world from a different viewpoint, and it offered me a chance to show myself and the world what I was made of.

CHAPTER 6

MINISTERS AND
TRIGGERMEN

I expected I'd stick out as the only black officer on the Fostoria police force, so it didn't come as a shock to experience some racial discrimination. What shocked me was where most of it came from.

"Oh, here comes the token."

Samuel. We'd had words before.

At that time, Toledo had a big gang problem, and some of the wannabes would come down to Fostoria, a forty-five minute or so drive away, and hang out at the projects. Samuel had been involved in several shootings and was trying to establish himself as a gangster, the leader and man of the town.

I approached the group of ten to twelve young black men who were milling around in the parking lot of the bowling alley across the street from one of the projects. Several other officers arrived about the same time I did.

"You just trying to show off 'cause of that badge and everything," Samuel said.

My chest and face felt hot, and something inside me rose up. I kept my cool, pretending it didn't affect me.

"They only hired you because they had to have one, because you look token," he went on.

I don't think Samuel or any of the other black people I heard that from believed that was true, but the fact that they would say it and try to belittle me in front of other officers pissed me off.

The other officers went about their business.

We'd been called to the scene to break up a fight, but when we got there those involved had worked through their issue or decided to focus their anger on an outsider. And who better than the outsider cop?

I was grateful that my fellow officers let me handle my business.

On one level, Samuel was right: I was an officer of the law. Because of the badge, I couldn't deal with him the way a lot of men handle things, the way I might otherwise have handled him were it not for lessons learned at home. By default, I'd learned early to "use my words" and that the tongue can hurt more than fists and leave a scar deeper than any knife wound. It's a lesson Samuel seemed to have picked up on, too.

When I was in high school, Glenda and I got into it one afternoon. We were standing in the middle of the living room arguing. Who knows what we were fighting about, but we were definitely fighting. I punched her in her leg. I hit her so hard I thought I'd broken her leg. She screamed at the top of her girl lungs, and wouldn't you know it was one of the times our dad was home. He beat the holy mess out of me. It was not the usual father-son teaching moment. This was man-to-man, a graduate-level class from The School of Moore and its headmaster. From that day on, I never laid my hands on another woman.

Don't hit women was the lesson of the day, but what I learned going forward was how to stand up for and defend myself with my mind and mouth—without using profanity.

"*Token.*" This wasn't about police work now. I wasn't going to let this jackass punk me out like that. I had no leverage, nothing I could arrest him for. And like I always tell young cops, don't threaten people. You've got to be careful about what you say because if you tell somebody you're going to arrest them and then you walk away, that will spread through the town quicker than I've ever been able to run.

I walked right into the middle of the crowd and approached the thick body with the mouth. I stepped right up to Samuel. I tilted my head down and looked him right in the eye. We were so close I could've put my tongue out and touched his nose. Eyeball to eyeball I said, "You know what Samuel?"

He didn't say or do anything.

"You know what," I continued. "I finally realize why you don't like me." I paused but kept my eyes on his.

"Why?" he said after a few seconds.

I stepped a fraction of an inch closer and said, "Because you can't whoop me."

We stood there staring at each other for several more seconds. A few low "Ooooo"s reached our ears. He didn't make a move. Now the shot had been fired. He and I both knew that any shot fired back would probably give me the ammunition I didn't have when I first approached him. He surprised me with his silence and restraint, but maybe that was due to me shocking him with my aggressive and personal verbal challenge.

The left corner of my mouth curved up just a bit; I tipped my chin up, turned, and walked away. The other men around him made it clear that he wasn't the man of the town he thought himself to be. He was playing a part, and everyone saw him for the actor he was.

Our paths crossed again when I responded to a true shots-fired call. When I arrived, Samuel was lying on the ground bleeding from a fresh gunshot wound to the leg. For a reason that is lost in the haze of memory, taking him to the hospital by ambulance wasn't the most expedient choice. He wasn't mortally wounded, so I helped him into my cruiser and rushed him to the nearest ER. No words were exchanged this time.

Later, an officer said, "Dude, what were you doing? You should've just waited for the ambulance, and taken your sweet time."

If you pay attention, it doesn't take long to realize that most people who mouth off or act out do so not out of true spite but because they're mad, or high, or scared. I'd sometimes see people days and even months after an unpleasant exchange and they would be cordial to me. They'd say, "Hey man, I'm sorry about that." I'd just say, "No problem, man," and would try to exchange a little small talk. Samuel was an exception.

No matter the context, words matter. They are powerful in and of themselves, and they determine our actions and how others interact with us, both as individuals and as a group.

While at a football game in the early '90s, I overheard an exchange that has stuck with me for decades.

I was sitting behind a group of parents—white parents—when some kids approached.

Amused by something she saw, one of the parents said, "Look at this group," and nodded toward the kids. White kids.

Later, more kids approached. "Oh God. Here comes a gang," someone said. The comment wasn't addressed to me. I looked in the direction the speaker was looking. Coming down the stadium walkway was a group of six or seven eleven- or twelve-year old kids. Normal kids, same as the first. But black kids.

Group. Gang. I hadn't thought myself naïve but that totally blew me away.

"Sticks and stones can break my bones, but words can never hurt me," is a rhyme for children, very young children. Very early we all learn the power of words and symbols and where we stand in relation to what is considered good and what is considered bad. The author Robin DiAngelo talks about how "racially coded language" is still part of our vernacular, even in policing. We use words "such as 'urban,' 'inner city,' and 'disadvantaged,' but rarely use 'white' or 'over-advantaged' or 'privileged.'"[1] Words can wound or they can heal and when used carelessly, sticks, stones, and broken bones among other things can follow. When I speak to young people, I talk about this, about the power of association and how it shapes and deforms our perception of the world around us, and can precondition us to make poor, even devastating decisions no matter what color their skin is.

* * *

"Your shifts are starting. Get out of my briefing room. You know where you're supposed to be. Stop talking and get out there." Our shift supervisor was in a tizzy, and I didn't feel like listening anymore. I grabbed my keys and headed out the door. I swung into my car and pulled out of the lot heading north.

Moments later, the police radio went off. Shots fired. About thirty seconds later, I came up on a guy who'd just shot up a cash register, an armed robbery in progress. He was within a hundred yards of me, about the length of a football field away. Cash register in hand, he froze. I looked through the windshield and swear I could see the whites of his eyeballs. They matched the color of his skin. I felt him looking right into my eyes too. He dropped the register, ran across the street, and jumped a fence. I pulled up, slammed the cruiser into park, jumped the fence, and ran after him. He went around a corner. When I came around the corner just seconds later, he took out a gun and pointed it right at me. I unholstered my service weapon and pointed it at him.

"Freeze. Drop it!"

I could've shot him. I would've been totally justified. He had already fired his weapon at the cashier, and here he stood threatening to shoot an officer of the law. Instead, he threw his gun down and ran. I re-holstered my gun, ran after and caught him. Then I went back and recovered his weapon. He must've been one of the few perps in town who didn't know that he couldn't outrun Officer Clayton Moore. That would never have happened had it not been for our supervisor harping on us to leave the station. I was in the right place at the right time.

In all my years as a police officer, I never had to fire my weapon at a suspect. I had to pull it a couple of times, but never fired it outside of routine firearms training and recertifications.

The first time I pulled my gun had taught me a valuable lesson that likely saved that dude's life.

Late one night in the early '90s my good friend and partner, Officer Bill Brenner, and I were doing routine building checks, making sure doors were locked on certain buildings because people had been breaking in and stealing stuff. While we were doing that, we got a call that somebody was in one of the buildings. We went there and almost immediately saw a man. The only thing between us was a window.

Brenner and I yelled at the guy, "Get your hands up ... where we can see them!"

The guy didn't comply. It was intense. We were yelling and screaming at him," Get your hands up! Put your hands up!"

The suspect bent as if to kneel and then reached for something in his boot.

I said, "He has a gun. He has a gun," then "Drop it, don't do it!" But I held steady. I hadn't seen a weapon. I wasn't going to flinch until I did. Even if I had seen a weapon, my next command would have been exactly what I told the cash register suspect: "Drop your weapon."

He didn't have a gun. He had bent down to stash his dope in his shoes.

I could've shot him as soon as he reached for his boot, and I would be in the same predicament as every other cop who's ever shot an unarmed suspect and been called to account. I hadn't seen a weapon, but I could have said I saw him reach for one or what I thought was one. It was dark after all. But we didn't know, and we weren't going to shoot until we did.

Even though other officers I worked with could make the claim of never having shot a suspect, the perception that a peaceful solution was always the highest priority wasn't how some would-be gangbangers saw things. One older officer in particular was known for his less than level-headed ways. When I first heard someone refer to him, I asked, "Who's Trigger?" Everyone around me laughed and one of them said, "You know that dude that's always pulling his gun."

On calls, sometimes I'd say, "Okay I'll tell you what, y'all gonna listen to me, if not, I'll just call Trigger down here."

"Come on man, don't be doing that. Don't be calling him down here."

Police and military work attract people who enjoy having power over others. What greater power is there than being able to take the life of another human being from a distance, knowing that if it happens during the commission of a crime or even a suspected crime that you'll be insulated from the consequences?

When cops behave that way, it paves the way for bad civilian behavior, just like seeing a cop speeding without his lights on is seen as tacit approval for other drivers to speed.

I get so pissed when I hear about police officers shooting unarmed civilians, and it makes me sick to think about what happened to Trayvon Martin and the fact that George Zimmerman was acquitted of all charges—that his actions were seen as justified self-defense. Really? He was being the aggressor. He was chasing Martin around, but somehow his actions are justified even to the point of taking a young man's life.

When we talk to kids in school, we tell them that before getting into a fight, you must first try flight. You must try to run away from the fight. If you don't, if violence is your first reaction, you'll get suspended. Zimmerman could have fled. He didn't have to chase Trayvon. But according to a probable cause affidavit, he chased him and chased him. He followed him. He was on a mission. He was exercising his authority, small and unofficial as it was.[2]

The affidavit also contains witness testimony about Zimmerman's statements, which include evidence of profiling. There's no doubt in my mind that if Trayvon Martin had been white, that tragedy wouldn't have happened.

When I consider the trigger-happy cops I've known and those I've heard about, patterns emerge. Mentality, traits, and qualities overlap. Why?

Let's look at these people. Let's do more background studies on officers who have been involved in shootings. There's nothing wrong with that. The FBI doesn't take just anyone. We need higher standards in police departments.

But I'm not talking about targeting police officers or singling them out. Let's also do the same thing with minorities who have been involved in shootings. Let's find out if they have similar traits and qualities that law enforcement officers and quasi-law enforcers who've pulled weapons and shot someone have. Maybe then we could say that it's not a white or black thing but a something-else thing, something we can detect early and educate and redirect. And at the first sign that an officer is trigger happy, we can take bold measures to sanction behavior and protect the public. Police academy training that emphasizes watching a suspect's hands and feet just isn't cutting it, and the job is dangerous enough without some hothead getting into the mix.

* * *

Domestic calls are among the most dangerous types of calls an officer responds to. They can also be some of the most mentally and emotionally challenging, and even funny, when everything is said and done.

"Did she do that to you?" I asked as I approached the couple I assumed I'd been dispatched to deal with. I tilted my head toward the woman who still had the phone in her hand.

The man had scratches all over him. I thought, *Wow, she scratched the mess outta you, dog,* but I stayed in officer mode. The guy was upset but keeping his cool.

"What happened?" I asked him.

He told me his side of the story. They'd gotten into it, and she'd gotten up in his face. He'd pushed her off himself, and she'd broken loose on him. It wasn't his idea to call the cops, though. It was hers.

"Is that what happened?" I asked her.

Her story matched his on all major points. Often the stories differ radically, in which case an officer is left to wonder who to believe. Before the O.J. Simpson trial and the attention to domestic violence that it brought, officers had some discretion in situations like these. After the Simpson trial, if we got called out on a domestic, someone was going to jail. Most often the man.

"Okay, got it," I said to her. I pulled out my cuffs and continued, "At this point we're gonna charge you with domestic violence, you have the right—"

"What do you mean charge *me*?"

She started screaming and dancing around, "He pushed me, he's the man, he ..."

Technically, he had put his hands on her. He'd even put his hands on her first, but she didn't have a mark on her, and her story didn't indicate that he'd been violent.

We tried to finish reading her rights, but she went berserk, screaming, crying, bawling, and everything. At that point, we stopped talking, cuffed her, and loaded her in the car because she wasn't going to listen to us anyhow. She carried on while we drove directly to the station. Before we processed her, we started over and gave her the Miranda warning.

In most cases, even when the female is the aggressor and the male the victim, her blows don't leave marks. And in most cases, it's the female who calls 911. But in many cases, it's impossible to determine aggressor from victim, but someone has to go to jail. My dad had pounded the never-hit-a-woman-lesson into me, but it was still hard to stand there and try not to think, *Dude, you should've just popped her a good one rather than let her mess you up like that.* The other part of me knew that flight, removing himself from the situation, was what he should have done.

However, that could have been interpreted as fleeing the scene of a crime, especially if he didn't have a mark on him, which would have compounded the charges he would have faced. There are no if-this, then-this rules to live by. There are double standards. And some laws, written with good intentions, inadvertently harm groups of people. Domestic violence laws are for women; it's that simple. When police officers lost the ability to assess the situation based on their knowledge of those involved and all the evidence, some people are unfairly penalized.

There were times, usually after hours, when a guy had been drinking or doing drugs and his wife or girlfriend would call. We'd show up and have to make an arrest. Sometimes the female would even say in front of the male that she wanted us to arrest him. We'd arrest the guy, and the woman would get combative and try to interfere with the arrest. Much like my threat to call old Trigger down, it was a threat. All she wanted was us to come down and make him stop whatever he was doing, and just tell him to quit it.

When the woman gets combative and we have to try to subdue her, the guy says, "Get your hands off my wife," and then you've got a fiasco on your hands. You go there to solve one problem but end up having two problems, and things can go from one to two in a heartbeat.

To compound the problem, officers know that an arrest can cost a person their job. Financial pressures are one of the main things people fight over and can be both an underlying cause of drug and alcohol abuse and domestic violence. By arresting a person and threatening future income, what might be a minor scrap can snowball into a massive familial issue that actually makes matters worse for the victim. It's a no-win.

Unfortunately, those calls do tend to come more from minority communities than white ones. What *is* the same is how people of every race and gender threaten cops with lawsuits. White people express a sense of entitlement in these cases, as if they are somehow above the law or that because it was "a one-time thing" or "first offense" they're somehow immune. Minorities, on the other hand, throw around the phrase "police brutality."

That's why it's so important, even though it can feel like death by a thousand paper cuts, to cross your *t*'s and dot your *i*'s. There's nothing like having evidence—a good paper trail and being able to connect the dots. It can help put out a lot of fires. Just do what you need to do. It comes back to officers needing to know what they can and can't do, what they can and can't say, and then how they go about their day-to-day job serving the people, not managing or ruling over them. That's what I always tried to do, which is why I was so surprised when I was passed over three times for the Officer Friendly position.

* * *

Around 1995, the Officer Friendly of Safety Town, a community liaison position, came open, and I applied. Chief Mason turned me down. I was too green, Mason said. A more experienced officer was better suited for the role. I was disappointed and confused. I let it go. I knew it would open up again the next year, and it would be mine.

A year later, I applied for the second time. I advised the chief that I had years of experience and was one of only two people in the department with a four-year college degree. "It's an appointed position," he replied, "Years of experience and education don't really play a role." He denied my request again. I was confused and angry.

The third time I applied, I was granted the summer position. The summer lasted until I left the Fostoria police force. To this day, no matter where I go in town, I'm called by several names: Officer Friendly, Friendly, Mr. Friendly. I'm called these names by the kids (now grownups) in the class, the junior instructors that were in the class, and their parents. I'm tagged for life, but it's a label I happily live with.

Things were looking up on the job front, and I planned to take the sergeant's exam.

CHAPTER 7

UNFINISHED BUSINESS

*N*o. No. No. No. No. Not today!

It was just before 6:00 p.m. I was running late; the train was running early. I sat at the blinking railroad stop tapping my steering wheel and chastising myself for taking those few extra minutes to do last-minute studying.

Four minutes after the exam was scheduled to begin, I walked through the classroom door. Pat Brooks was in his seat filling in his personal information on the first page just like everyone else. I hadn't missed anything. Whew, happy birthday to me, I thought as I closed the door behind me.

"You're late," the commissioner said.

I went to take my seat at the only empty desk with an exam lying face down.

"Don't even sit down, Moore."

The heat rose up in neck. Before I could figure out what to say, he continued. "I'm sorry, but the rules state that once the exam begins only those in the room at that time are permitted to take it."

"I got stuck behind a train on the way in. Here I am. Y'all haven't started."

Everyone in the room was quiet. Nobody stood up for me by saying that they didn't have a problem with me taking the test since it hadn't started yet. I stood there in shock for a minute. Not one for conflict or drama, I walked out. I looked at the walls on my way out and said to myself, "Happy birthday to me."

I don't know which was worse, knowing that Brooks, who was an excellent test taker but not as good a cop as me, would now leapfrog me, or not getting the pay bump I really needed.

* * *

It was the mid-nineties, but Denise hadn't shaken the Material Girl ethos of the eighties. We were still together and had just bought a house, a new car, and new furniture. My wife had also recently left her job at Whirlpool to take a lower paying job that would allow her the flexibility to pursue her dream of starting a business. I'd been support- ive, but when she came to me with a plan to take a trip, I said, "You know, we purchased all these things based on two incomes. When you left your good job to go to this other job where you're making less …well, less is less. We can't continue to spend out."

Unlike my family with a lot of mouths to feed and not a whole lot to go around, Denise is the only child of two parents who'd always had good jobs. She'd never gone without and didn't have any desire to start now.

"Clayton, it's Vegas, not Sydney or Paris. It's not that big a deal." She was mad.

"It's not a big deal to your parents. They've got money, and it's just them now. We don't have money, *and* we have kids. Your aunt and uncle are going, but it's just them too. Some of your cousins are going, but I don't know their situation. Just because they're all going doesn't mean we have to go."

She sat down on the sofa without much more than a nod and pulled her thin legs up under her body. She looked like a dejected little kid who'd been told she couldn't go to a sleepover when everybody else got to go.

"Let me think about it and see what I can figure out," I said. I turned and left, already knowing what it would take.

I worked a second job while Denise and her family planned the big trip. Maybe not a big trip by other people's standards, but there were a lot of people on the list. At least I'd be going with people I really loved.

Vegas in July. Four days of high stakes were in front of us.

We were all laughing and having a great time. Everything was fine. We were in the casino of our hotel, just doing what family and Vegas tourists do. After loitering for a while, I decided I needed a bit more action, so I walked away and sat down at a table not far away.

"Hey cuz, what are you doing over here?" A few of Denise's cousins were coming up beside me.

"Playing blackjack," I said.

One of the two said, "Hey can you teach me how to play?"

"Yeah, yeah." I motioned for her to sit beside me and started teaching her the rules of the game.

Not long after we'd started, Denise stepped up to the table. "Why are you spending more time with my cousin than you are with me?" For other couples, this might have been a joke, sexy banter even. Not for us, and she'd said it loud enough for anyone within fifteen feet to hear. A knot started to form in the pit of my stomach.

"You've got to be kidding me?" I said. "I walked away because everybody was doing something, and I was basically left out on my own. I just come over here to play blackjack. And when I left, people followed me."

Her cousin, my student, looked around. Clearly unsure of what to say or do, she just stood there awkwardly.

I continued. "We're playing blackjack in front of all these people. We're laughing and everything. This is your cousin! What's your problem?" Denise didn't answer. She just turned and walked away, leaving the three of us at the blackjack table to figure out how to recapture the fun. I really didn't want to hear any more about this, so I lost a couple of hands on purpose.

"Y'all are bringing me bad luck," I said. I laid my cards down and pushed my chair back. "I'm going to another table."

I went farther away this time, all the way to the other side of the room. I found a table tucked away out of plain sight and started over. Ten minutes later, a bunch of cousins found me and sat at the same table again.

"Cuz, we're going to change your luck," one of them said. Denise wasn't with them, so they were off to a good start, but I was really trying to accommodate my wife; my luck wouldn't hold with any female cousins in the mix. We had a great time, and there was no more drama for the rest of the day.

The following day at around three in the afternoon, we all gathered for dinner. There were a dozen or more of us around the table talking about what we'd done the day before and what we were about to eat.

One of Denise's cousins looked up from her menu and said, "Oh yeah, Clayton, happy birthday!"

"Thank you, Shelia. You're the first one to tell me that today."

That was the best gift anyone could have given me. Clarity.

As other people chimed in their best wishes, I stepped away from the moment. Looking over at Denise, I thought, *This woman doesn't care about me. She does not care about me at all. Everything I did to bust my butt to get her out here with her family because that's what she wanted, and she can't even say, 'Hey, happy birthday' on my birthday.*

She didn't know it, but that was the end. Before dinner was over, I had analyzed my options, considered the counter moves, and had outlined my escape plan.

I went back home, opened a separate account, and started saving money because I knew I had to get a house. I wanted at least three to four months' rent money, and I knew I had to buy my girls a bedroom suite so they'd each have their own bed. All the arrangements were made so that when I moved out, it would be a smooth transition. The only thing I couldn't control was what Denise would do with the girls, the one thing she'd know she could use to hurt me.

Nine months after our trip to Vegas, we were having the same argument we'd had since before Vegas.

"I can only say I'm sorry so many times. I cut off the relationship. I went to counseling. I'm not going to live every day with you bashing and throwing this at me and trying to beat me down like I'm nobody," I said. "We all make mistakes, poor decisions, whatever you wanna call them."

Denise huffed but didn't say anything. Her wounded lover bit had long since gotten stale.

"Listen, I'm not going to stay here." I said. "I'm leaving."

That got her attention. "I don't want to file," I said. "If you want to file, that's fine. I'm not trying to embarrass you or belittle you or anything like that, but I'm not staying here. I'm just not happy, Denise."

She finally spoke. "Well you go ahead and file."

"Denise, listen. I'm dead serious. I'm going to file for that."

"No. File. Go ahead!"

"Okay, fine. Where do you want to be served the papers at?"

"Doesn't matter to me." Her voice was calm, but I knew she was seething.

"Denise, where ... do ... you ... want ... to ... be ... served ... the papers at?"

She never would tell me where and when she'd like to be served the papers. In the end I did file, and when she was served, the shit hit the fan. She underestimated my will and willingness to go through hell to protect myself and live the life I wanted.

In 1996, my first marriage was over. My girls were confused and angry. It took a long time to rebuild those relationships and to let adulthood experiences catch up with the information they were given at the time. I'm grateful that my girls and I can have open conversations about our lives and lessons learned. Just the other day, one of them came to me with a problem she associated with a poor choice. She'd already come to terms with it and was moving forward to correct course, but she still felt the sting.

"Listen," I said. "Don't look at it like it was a poor decision. Those things are only poor decisions if you continue to make them and don't learn—then they're poor decisions. This is just a life growing event you're going through. You learn from it, you grow, and if you grow, you become a better person. It's that simple ... and if you get stuck not knowing what to do, that's okay. Remember what I always say—"

"I know, Daddy. There's more than one way to skin a cat." I could almost hear her eyes rolling, but I had to smile.

I loved my dad but he hadn't have the time to spend with me that I had with my girls, but in the time we did have, Dad had given me life lessons that I could pass down.

One summer morning, my dad had broken my usual routine of getting up and immediately running off to play sports with the neighbor kids. We often wouldn't come home until dark, but on this morning my dad had other plans for me.

As I was crossing the threshold headed out, he said, "No, you're going to learn how to change a tire today, a tire on a car."

"I don't want to change no tire on no car. I want to go play football or basketball or baseball." (Of course, I said this to myself.) My friends were waiting and changing a tire was the last thing I wanted to do. I may have been able to talk my way out of it, who knows, but even if I had, my pout sealed my fate.

"Stand right there," he said pointing to a spot on the driveway far enough away from the car that I could take everything in. "Just watch me."

He hiked up the thighs of his pant legs and squatted down beside the front driver-side tire. He'd already laid out all the proper tools but struggled to get the tire off.

"Come over here and help me, son." He handed me a tool, but I couldn't do any better than what he'd done.

"This is impossible!" I said.

And then my dad said something I've never forgotten, "Sonny boy, there's more than one way to skin a cat." That kind of sums up every challenge we face in life right there. We found a way to get the wheel nuts off and proceeded to change the tire.

Sports has taught me a lot about will and resiliency, but my dad is the one who taught me to think strategically, to consider problems from every angle and see them for what they are—just puzzles to work out and overcome. It's something I tell my real kids as well as my sports kids: If something doesn't go your way, don't give up. Try another way.

My dad may not have been there for the little, day-to-day stuff when I was growing up, but he was there. I wasn't prepared for him not being there.

"I know you and Mommy want to go back to North Carolina," I said to him one afternoon.

He looked up at me from his chair in the living room.

I went on. "We're going to get you a house there and everything."

I was still on the police force but had also started taking classes to pursue a law degree. I was seeing a future in civilian life and thinking that maybe I really could be one of those kids who helps support his parents financially.

Just a week before, I'd come home and gotten the news that he'd been life-flighted to Toledo Hospital. All those years of driving a cab and not doing much else had caught up to him.

"I'm sorry. Your dad has a total blockage. There's nothing we can do," the doctor had said. "Due to his age and poor health, we can't risk surgery."

A few days later, my dad went home, and now we were sitting in the living room talking about the future. He'd been looking better since returning home. It was nice to just sit and talk. I was glad he was going to be okay. I hadn't been able to think of the alternative when the doctor gave us his prognosis.

"I've got to head out soon, Dad. Need anything before Mommy and I go?"

"Make sure you take care of your brother."

"Yeah, I'm going to take care of Damon, Daddy."

Dad was supposed to have been going with us but still wasn't strong enough, so my mom and I were headed to Columbus to see Damon play for Ohio State. Ava, who lived next door to our parents, stayed home in case Dad needed anything.

At some point during Damon's game, Dad started having severe chest pains. Ava called 911. When a friend of ours, a nurse, heard who the call was about, she rushed over to my parents' house. The ambulance team sped him to the nearest hospital, but the doctor had been right. There was nothing anyone could do.

Mom and I got the call not long after the game ended. I hadn't even talked to my mom about what was going on with Dad. None of us thought or acted like he was really on his way out of our lives, or maybe we just couldn't accept it. Even that morning talking to him, I hadn't had a clue. We're a tight family. "Take care of your brother" hadn't struck me as anything but a thing to say before I left. Now I wondered if Dad knew, if he didn't want us to stick around because he wanted us to live and enjoy each other in the way we'd planned. Maybe he didn't want to put my mom through watching him go. I don't know. I will never know.

We walked through the stadium parking lot in shock. It was October 4, 1997. Daddy was gone.

* * *

In 1997, my brother the All-American collegiate athlete, Damon Moore, was drafted by the Philadelphia Eagles. He was getting his shot at the big time, the National Football League—the shot I'd always wanted but would never get. I might have been jealous had we not been so close, but I'd coached him and tutored him and been there to watch and help him get to the moment when he put on a team jersey and a team cap not as a fan but as a player, as a man who'd done the hard things and who'd earned his place.

One of the last things my father said to me was, "Take care of your brother." I was going to.

There are times in life when looking back I can see how unbeknownst to me I've been working toward something my entire life, or that God has been directing me toward something. This was one of them. My fascination with sports and respect for Ali and Cosell. My love of the law and legal language. Contracts and negotiation. Finance and strategic planning.

About a year before Damon got drafted, one of my law professors had us watch "Jerry Maguire," a movie about a conflicted sports agent, starring Tom Cruise. In a fit of conscience, superstar agent Jerry Maguire distributes to dozens of other agents a hastily written call for more humanity and less avarice. The open praise his colleagues heap on him and the adoration of a lonely, attractive young mother blind him to the fact that he'd signed his own professional death warrant. Only one client sticks, a client whose career is on the skids, but whose personal relationships flourish. Both men must navigate the cutthroat system while learning to work together and bring their heads and their hearts into alignment to succeed personally and professionally. Jerry must learn that the superficial skills that brought him success in his professional life don't serve him in romantic relationships, and that the vulnerability he showed when writing his manifesto is required for true depth and love in a relationship.

Sitting there watching, I cycled through all the emotions. Goose bumps came and went, and in the final scenes, hot tears welled in my eyes. I thought, *Yes!* That was my dream job. Those were my dream relationships.

Soon after, I became a certified NFL Players Association Agent. I wasn't interested in representing Damon. As his brother, I was interested in learning everything I could about the system he was playing in and everything he needed to know and would be responsible for improving. I wanted to be prepared to assist him in anything he'd need help with in the future.

While working the midnight shift as a police officer, going to law school, coaching high school athletes and community-organized teams, raising my girls, and working my way out of a marriage that no longer made sense in my head or my heart, I learned all I could about the stock market and the experience of professional football players on and off the field. I was a certified NFLPA agent for two years but was overextended. Dealing with the grief of losing my dad made the weight of everything I was trying to carry even heavier.

I was doing too many things. And when we do too many things, the little things don't get done the way they're supposed to. I'd love to say that I recognized that at the time and made the decision to drop out of law school before it was too late and balls started dropping, but the reality is that the decision was made for me. My grades dropped to a point where I knew I wouldn't be able to recover and stay on track while also managing my life and things I had to do as a father and responsible member of society. I had to walk away from law school like I'd walked away from pursuing my dream of being a professional football player.

The divorce was hell. Denise did everything she could to establish herself as the sole victim and me as the villain. My relationship with the girls was collateral damage. In many ways, the next few years were lonely for me and messed with my sense of self-worth. One of my primary drivers—to be the kind of great dad who was always there to see and support his children—was pre-empted by the complications of divorce.

On the upside, the extra time allowed me to refocus. In 1999, I went back to school and earned a paralegal degree. I had my head on straight again. I was dealing with things. I'd kept it all together and earned a 4.0 GPA.

I was elected president of the patrolmen's union. Things were looking up. I was back on the right side of life. Life and work moved along relatively smoothly for the next several years, until the fall of 2004 when things took a turn for the worse, and later in 2008, my personal and professional life came to a screeching halt.

CHAPTER 8

THE WRONG SIDE OF THE NEW LAW

In 2004, Chief Day was fired.[1] Per standard protocol, a "competitive examination" was offered. Two eligible candidates from within the Fostoria force took the exam. Of the two, Phil Hobbs met the eligibility requirements and was our acting police chief for ten months before deciding the role wasn't a great fit. The way many of us saw it, Mayor Davoli took that opportunity to recreate the Fostoria Police Department in his own image.

Neither the patrolmen's union, of which I was still president, nor the Ohio Patrolmen's Benevolent Association (OPBA), of which I'd later become president, were keen to see their members and fellow officers passed over in favor of someone hand-picked from the outside, which is exactly what we felt happened when Davoli appointed John McGuire in February of 2006.

McGuire came in slick as a snake. Where Brooks was loud, McGuire was quiet—sneaky, phony, and conceited. He was fairly young, in his mid-thirties and took special care to always look good. He may have looked good, but it didn't take long for many to come to see him as inept and there to serve the mayor, not the people.

The role of a union is to protect workers' rights by opposing abuses of power and unfair limitations on advancement and access to fair wages. The patrolmen's union and the OPBA agreed that by not promoting from within, the City of Fostoria was violating the rights of officers and operating outside the statutes. McGuire's style and low job I.Q. didn't help the situation. Within months, the unions filed a court claim to remove McGuire from his position. In August 2006, the appellate court determined the appointment of Chief McGuire to be unlawful, but the city and McGuire weren't ready to let it go. The case went all the way to the Ohio Supreme Court.

In addition to the unions' claim that the hiring of McGuire was unlawful, many felt that even if his appointment was within the city's rights, McGuire himself wasn't qualified. Officers began to do some digging, and conversations about our acting leader went something like this:

"You're not going to believe this."

"Hit me."

"He either can't spell or he's a liar."

"What are you talking about?"

"Check this out ... on this one he spells his name M-C-G-U-I-R-E, but look at the spelling on this one, M-A-C-G-U-I-R-E. Do you think it was an accident or some kind of false identity and he forgot how he'd decided to spell his name?"

One point of concern was his degree, which turned out to be an offshore mail-order degree. It was the kind of deal where you plug in your past education and experience and the system assigns values and spits out a degree.

"Hey, plug in one of the dogs and see what happens!"

It was funny, but none of us really expected the results that our K-9 officer got: He scored higher than our human Chief McGuire. We—the union—added the K-9 officer to the witness list. A judge later removed him from the list but not before the people at the *Late Night with David Letterman* show got wind of it, and the dog got his fifteen minutes of fame.

At this point, there was an us-versus-them mentality. Things were getting hot.

In early 2007, having taken and passed the exam, I was promoted to sergeant. That slot had become available because Scott Miller, a good friend of mine, resigned from the police force due to allegations of misconduct. The general feeling was that McGuire had been brought in to be a hatchet man. Nobody involved in the union felt safe. The city, for reasons that started long before this, seemed to think the union and its members weren't playing on the same team. What some at the city didn't seem to understand was that the union presidents and vice presidents are the voice of everybody they represent. Whether they agreed with a union member's claim or not, when they speak to the media or draft memos and other documents, they are the members' active agents. That's their job. That was my job—right up my alley thanks to my protective nature and sports agent training.

On July 28, 2008, we all got the answer we'd been waiting for. The Ohio Supreme Court ruled in favor of the city.[2]

McGuire had won. But winning against the union wasn't enough; he seemed hell-bent on ridding the ranks of his perceived enemies, starting with those whose names appeared on the court filings—all of us except Brooks that is. When my time came, I wasn't surprised.

Not long after McGuire won his case, I became the subject of a lengthy investigation. McGuire gave me a three-day suspension. I filed a grievance about this disciplinary action and was completely vindicated.[3] Having lost that round, McGuire waited for his next opportunity to strike.

* * *

At that time I was acquainted with Fostoria's Law Director, Timothy Hoover. We didn't usually talk much, so when I stepped out of the station into the refreshingly cold November air and he said, "Hey, Moore. How's it going?" I figured we'd exchange the usual pleasantries and I'd be on my way.

"Oh, hey, Hoover, I'm fine. You?"

He pushed his thick glasses up his nose and took another long pull on his cigarette.

"I'm alright, thanks." He paused, flicked some ash into the smoking bucket, glanced toward the doors and continued. "It's kind of crazy around here lately."

"Yeah, crazy is right."

The conversation drifted for a few minutes before settling squarely on our by-now-not-so-new chief of police and his loyal assistant, Klitzer.

"Those two are pretty chummy," I said. "She's not exactly someone I trust."

"Maybe," Hoover grunted as he crushed out one cigarette in the sand. As he pulled another from his pack, I stepped off the curb and toward my car. I swung my gym bag over my left shoulder, and as I turned to go said, "I wouldn't get too cozy with McGuire is all I'm sayin'."

He didn't say anything but tipped his chin at me and smiled as put the cigarette in his mouth and pulled his lighter from his coat pocket.

"Goodnight, man," I said and stepped into the dimly lit parking lot. By the time I pulled into my driveway, the conversation was long behind me.

In the past, we'd had captains and sergeants on each shift, but because it's a small department, McGuire did away with the captain position. Our two captains became administrative captains running the day shift, and the sergeants now ran the shifts. In January of 2008, I was the supervising sergeant on the midnight shift. It was a setup that worked just fine for me.

"Sit down, Moore." McGuire ushered me into his office and pointed to an ugly metal chair shoved into the corner of his office.

He sat down behind his desk and slid a neatly stacked pile of papers to one side. I slid the chair over in front of his desk, sat, and tried to hide my disdain.

"I'm transferring you to METRICH starting next week," he said. METRICH was a volunteer drug task force, a joint venture between several counties. It was run out of Tiffin, a small town about fifteen minutes outside Fostoria and a place I'd spent a fair amount of time in.

"But I didn't put in for that. That doesn't work for me. I can't work the afternoon shift. That's when I coach my kids." I got to see my girls regularly and was back coaching at the high school and couldn't be happier. That's where my heart was.

"It's not a request or suggestion, Clayton."

"But if you take me off mid shift, that messes with my custody arrangement and makes it hard for me to keep coaching in the afternoons."

"Well, I want to give my sergeants experience over there, rotate them every six months or so."

"So, there's nothing I can do to stay where I'm at?"

"No. I told you what I'm doing, and you're the most junior sergeant so I'm assigning you first. Make the necessary arrangements. I've already put in the paperwork. You'll be reporting to Chuck Boyer and Don Joseph."

"Yeah. I know Don." I got up and walked out.

This was one of the stupidest ideas I'd ever heard, taking experienced supervisors off shifts and rotating them every six months. One of the roles of task force members is to build their confidential informant (CI) lists. Six months is nothing in the drug world. You're not going to build those kinds of relationships and then suddenly walk away. The question of whether McGuire was incompetent or simply more concerned with screwing me over and keeping everyone on his enemy list off kilter wasn't something I could answer. Not that it mattered.

I had no choice. I reported as ordered to Tiffin.

On my way into METRICH in an undercover car, I stopped at a gas station in Tiffin to get something. As I walked through the door, the clerk looked up and said, "Hey, Clayton. How you doing? What are you doing over here?"

"Well, I'm doing fine," I said but thought, *Oh yeah, great idea. Put the only black cop in the area and lifelong resident on an undercover task force. You gotta be kidding me!* My stomach twisted as I tried to suppress my anger and fear. The job is hard enough—dangerous enough—without the people who are supposed to be looking out for our best interest putting us in situations that make us obvious targets.

There may have been a time when I would have embraced the added danger. Earlier in my career I'd been involved with entry team work doing drug raids and other heart-pumping types of calls. It was exciting to be a part of the sniper team. We'd gotten FBI training. Instead of going through the doors, we were the ones who'd get there early and be set up, overseeing things. We had our sniper rifles and covered the entry team. Every time we had a drug raid, I got an adrenaline rush. As a young cop, I wanted to be right in the middle of it. "Don't give me no cat in a tree call. Give me the action calls!" was a motto of sorts back then. But by 2008, I was settled. I was coaching and engaged to be married again. I was done with drama. I'd moved on.

Toward the end of my shift on my third day there, Don, Chuck, and I were sitting at our desks when Chuck said, "Hey, listen. We understand that you really didn't want to come over here, and we were hesitant about you coming because of that."

We talked about things, and I told them how I felt. Don and I already knew each other through my fiancée, Pam, and her kids. He knew all about my family and background, and the task force members who didn't know my family knew me because we'd run into each other often in the course of our work.

"If I can say this in confidence," I started. "This is crazy, ridiculous. It feels like a setup, but now I just have to go about it, you know?"

Everyone just took it all in. For the first time in a long time, I felt good about the people I was working with. Don and I were so much alike. It's not a surprise that we got along so well and have remained friends. He speaks his mind and isn't a pawn in anyone's game. He doesn't kiss anybody's butt, and if you don't like it, he don't care. Boyer was a decent guy but was getting close to retirement so wasn't into making waves.

We all ended up getting along well, and, having a zero-tolerance policy because of my older brother's issues when it comes to drugs, I did enjoy the work. But it's not where I wanted to be. I was past all that. If it was true that this would be only a six-month gig, I just wanted to get through it.

METRICH is all about drugs: making buys, surveillance, raids, searches and seizures. But those in that unit occasionally had to respond to the more pedestrian calls, like the call I got one day about a fight and lockdown at the local high school. It turned out to just be a verbal argument between a boyfriend and girlfriend. The lockdown was lifted, I stayed on site for the rest of the day, then went home. The work was more interesting most of the time though, and we'd often have "help."

Tiffin University, Heidelberg College, and Bowling Green State University were just a short drive from the METRICH office, and we'd occasionally have students who were studying law enforcement come and work as interns. One night, several of them went with us on a raid in Fostoria.

Having grown up there, I knew the town like the back of my hand. When I found out the address we were going to be watching, I called an old friend. We'd grown up and graduated together.

"Hey, man. It's Clayton."

We caught up for a few minutes, then I said, "Hey, listen. I'm on a job. It's right across the street from your house. We're gonna be using your driveway for this."

"Yeah, yeah. Clee, no problem."

On the night of the raid, Don and I walked out to our unmarked cars. I'd been talking to the interns, and Stephanie, the female intern, followed me and swung into the back-passenger seat of my vehicle as I got into the driver's seat. Don sat up front in the passenger seat. Later, on the way back to the office in Tiffin, Don rode in another vehicle and the intern sat up-front with me.

Before everything started, Stephanie and I had talked about what normally happens during these things.

"Most of the time, it's pretty routine, so don't worry about it. Just stay alert and watch."

It was dark when we pulled into the neighborhood, and I parked the car. While we were looking across the street at the house we were targeting, an informant was sent in to buy drugs. In addition to drugs, we knew there were weapons in the house. We had our informant wired and were recording the entire exchange. If something went down, we were prepared to rush in. There were unmarked cars and agents all over the area.

"What if someone comes out, sees us, and starts walking toward the car."

"Just act natural, I said. There's lots of reasons you could be sitting there, so don't assume anyone knows you're part of this. Just act natural."

Stephanie looked a little nervous but okay.

As we watched the buyer walk up to the house and before I got out of the car, I twisted in my seat and said, "Listen, come up here and sit in my seat. If you see people start coming toward the car, just play it off. Just act natural," I said and reached for the door handle.

"Well, what if they try to get in the car?" she asked.

"Keep the doors locked. If they have a gun or something, start the car and run their butt over, and get out."

Things went according to plan. It's not like these were high drama, but I did still get a little adrenaline spike, and it was fun to be there with the interns, remembering the thrill of my first times. On the way back to headquarters, I talked a thousand miles a minute. I talked about all kinds of things, football, police work, all kinds of stuff. I was just thrilled it had gone so well.

As we approached the METRICH building, I said, "You know, in regard to what you were saying earlier about, you know, what to do if they come at your window. I'm going to talk to Chuck about maybe having a guy and a girl together because we have guy interns too. If a guy and a girl were in a car together, they could act like boyfriend and girlfriend or something so the cover isn't blown, you know?"

"Yeah. Macking looks more natural than sitting in a car alone in the dark."

"Macking?"

"You know, macking…making out," she said.

"Okay. Whatever," I said, laughing as we got out of the car and headed into the building for our debrief.

Just another day at the office.

* * *

On what I thought was going to be another normal day, I'd gotten a call from my sister, Ava.

"Hey, sis. What's going on?"

"There's a warrant out for Damon."

"What?"

"Got in a bar fight or something stupid like that."

"Mommy okay?"

"Yeah. She's alright. Not happy but okay."

"Alright. I'll call you back."

I hung up with Ava and immediately dialed the Prosecutor's office.

"Hey, Carol. It's Clayton. How you doin'?"

Assistant Prosecutor Carol Reffner. We'd always had a good relationship. I'd testified many times in cases she'd been assigned to.

"Hi, Clayton. I'm good. Better than you, I'm guessing. I just got assigned to your brother's case."

"What's the charge?"

"Felonious assault ... it'd look good for him if he turned himself in."

"Any idea what the bail might be? What are the chances of this being an 'own-recognizance' thing?"

"Lemme take a look at it."

"Thanks, Carol. Appreciate it."

I hung up hoping for the best. I'd always liked Carol. Before becoming an attorney, she'd been a high school French teacher. She knew my mom and sisters, had known our whole family for years. Her husband and I even worked together. He'd been hired on as a cop after I was.

Later that day, I walked into the Fostoria Police Department with Damon.

"Damon, step this way, please. We need to get your side of the story." One of my fellow officers motioned Damon toward an interview room.

"Okay. I'm gonna leave the station while y'all do that. I'll see you later, Damon."

I received a call from my sister while at work later that day. She told me that Damon had been denied an OR bond and was taken to the county jail. She also said that a man had replaced Mrs. Reffner; I was later advised it was Hoover.

Two months later and while on task force duty, I was at the Seneca county courthouse with a few other METRICH guys for a case we were working on. Hoover was there for a reason related to another case. I hadn't seen him in a while and hadn't missed him. In fact, by then the sight of him was enough to piss me off. He walked over to our group and started talking to Boyer and a few of the other guys. I just hung back.

He wrapped up his conversation. As he stepped toward the door, he caught my eye and said, "Hey, can I talk to you?"

"Yeah, sure," I said. He motioned for me to follow him away from other people. We stepped into an adjoining room.

He hesitated and then asked, "How do you feel like … I mean, about what happened?"

He asked, so I answered. "No, you lied to me. You guys lied. What do you think? I'm pissed."

"Why do you feel we lied?"

"You know … I wasn't asking you not to give Damon a bond. That's not what I asked. I was asking one, if he was going to get OR'd and if not, what the bond was going to be so we could get the money out."

He didn't say much, so I kept going.

"That was all I asked. I wasn't asking you to give me no favors or do anything for him."

"Okay, well—"

"You couldn't even give me the courtesy of a heads-up so I could tell my mom and my sister and my brother what was really going on. You let all of us go down there thinking he'd be OR'd … We all came in and you did your thing and you know, basically you all lied. It's that simple."

He fumbled the pack of cigarettes in his pocket, nodded, and said, "Sorry you felt that way." He tried to go on with some BS excuse, but I cut him off.

"Whatever. You lied." I ended the conversation and walked out.

It was done. What did it matter now? I reconnected with the METRICH crew and went to lunch, putting it behind me. But not being kept in the loop with Damon wasn't the only thing I didn't know about. I was about to be hit with the biggest blindside of my career, perhaps my entire life.

CHAPTER 9

FIRED!

Not long after the courthouse conversation with Hoover, Chuck Boyer and Don Joseph called me into an office at METRICH.

"Hey, Clayton. Come in here for a minute, please," Chuck said.

He closed the door behind us, and we all stood facing each other. Chuck looked at Don before looking back over at me. "Hey, listen, he said. "I'm sure this will all get ironed out soon, but McGuire's calling you back to Fostoria."

"What are you talking about 'ironed out'?"

Don answered me. "After the undercover assignment with the interns, we got a sexual harassment complaint about you. It was investigated and McGuire knows there's no evidence of it, but he's calling you back to Fostoria for creating a hostile work environment."

A hostile work environment! McGuire is saying that I *created a hostile work environment?*

There really wasn't much more to say. All three of us knew that creating a hostile work environment is grounds for termination. This woman had handed McGuire a gift, and his slick self knew exactly what to do with it.

Chuck turned to open the door. As Don stepped past me and toward Chuck, he patted me on the shoulder and said, "Clayton, there's nothing to support the claim, and you're a good guy. Just go talk to McGuire and whoever else you need to over there, and get this thing behind you."

I gave him a pat on the back as he moved away from me. "Thanks, man," I said. At the moment, I was glad Chuck didn't say anything else because I'd expected him to stand up for me and at least look like he was in my corner. Instead, I felt like he was just being a politician, doing what he needed to do, not make any waves with McGuire so he could hold his position until he retired.

My stomach twisted at the thought of having to see McGuire's smug face and at the idea that Don, who'd become a good friend, had to be part of this.

In the moment, I didn't understand what was happening. In hindsight, I think it was a relative of the intern who was a law enforcement officer in a different county and known to be somewhat racist. I think he heard her talking about the entire discussion and convinced her to report it to Chief McGuire, or maybe he went straight to the chief, then the chief went to Boyer and Joseph and told them to look into it.

When McGuire pulled me from METRICH, he put me on day shift back at Fostoria PD where unbeknownst to me he was building a much bigger case against me. The incompetence of one of McGuire's closest allies offered an opportunity for him that I would never have expected.

Joanne Kitzler, a woman McGuire had worked closely with in the past and brought in to help him do his work—whatever work that may have been—had misplaced some paperwork related to a citation I'd issued. I had to go down and help her find it. She had no clerical skills. She was like a five-year-old trying to do an adult job. Turns out, the paperwork was on her desk. I huffed out of the building, got in my car, and rolled the window down before leaving.

Just as I was reaching to put the car in gear, Karen Nesbitt walked past.

Karen was one of the court bailiffs and a good friend of mine. She had lived right down the street from the church I go to. I'd invited her to come to church with me before and had been in her house. Our families were friends, and she and I knew a lot about each other, we'd had deep talks, and got along well.

"Hey, Clayton. What are you doing here?" she asked. She seemed genuinely happy to see me.

"Taking care of some stupid paperwork," I muttered.

"Clayton, what's wrong?"

"That freaking secretary—"

"What's going on?"

I told her what happened and then said, "I'm just gonna blow off some steam and roll."

She waved and I pulled out of the parking space and watched the building get smaller and smaller in my rearview mirror. I thought I'd put that incident behind me too, but I was about to have to face it again, and this time it was even bigger.

* * *

On April 30, 2008, McGuire called me into a meeting room.

"Moore, you know we take accusations of sexual harassment very seriously," McGuire said as he pulled up his chair and sat opposite me. I wanted to but didn't roll my eyes. I felt nothing but contempt, but tried to look cool, calm, and collected.

"The city has hired Arthur Marx to further investigate the sexual harassment claim made by Stephanie Dickson, and there is a separate incident in which you failed to advise the dispatcher of a traffic stop."

Marx sometimes worked on cases with us, but he wasn't in our department.

"What traffic stop? What are you talking about? Joseph and Boyer said there's nothing to the sexual harassment thing, and I have no idea what traffic stop you're talking about. I always call in my stops."

"Marx will fill you in on that later. What you need to understand is that starting today, I'm placing you on paid administrative leave until we sort all this out. Do you understand?"

"No, but yes. I don't understand what the problem is, but I get that you're putting me on leave."

McGuire informed me that I had seventy-two hours to submit a written statement. I went home, and on the second of May, I submitted a statement in writing.

* * *

Being on administrative leave didn't mean that I suddenly stopped getting calls from people in the community, people I'd been helping for years as a citizen and as a cop. One day, my phone rang.

"Hey, Clayton. It's Dave Parker." I'd known Dave for years.

"Hey, Dave. What can I do for you?"

"Well, I found a license plate and think it might belong to my son. I'd like to know if it's his."

Dave's son had been killed in a car accident, and he was still processing his grief.

"Yeah. Of course." I gripped the phone between my ear and shoulder and grabbed the nearest pen and piece of junk mail. "Okay, what's the number."

I wrote down the info and said, "Okay. Let me call this in and get back to you."

After hanging up, I dialed dispatch and asked the dispatcher to run it for me.

"Hang on one minute, Clayton. I just need to get permission since you're on administrative leave. Sorry, just hold on one second."

We called in plates all the time; I didn't expect any problems but held anyway.

"Sorry, Clayton. No can do. Brooks says no, you can't 'cuz of the leave thing."

Unbelievable!

"Fine," I said and hung up.

I called Dave back and told him he'd have to call the station and make the request himself.

* * *

A few weeks after being placed on administrative leave, I was told to report for a polygraph.

"You're gonna fail."

"I'm not gonna fail."

"Who's your guy?"

"Arthur Marx."

"Yeah you are. Don't do it. I'm telling you."

"I'll take a polygraph. I'm not a liar. I have nothing to lie about."

"Clayton, you *are* going to fail."

"What are you talking about, Scott?"

"Listen, when I took a polygraph to get on at the department, there were some things I didn't disclose, and I passed it. I was a little shocked … But when I had to take that polygraph before I got dismissed, I told the truth. I did not lie about one thing, and they said I failed it. They're going to make sure you fail this polygraph."

"Nah," I said. "Miller, trust me. You can't fail if you tell the truth. It's that simple."

Scott was right. I failed.

Marx prefaced his interview by saying, "Okay. Today, I'm going to ask you some questions about two events."

He asked me about the night of the drug bust and about what I'd said to the intern, and then he went down a completely different road.

"Have you ever taken drugs off anybody and not reported them?"

"Well, what do you consider drugs? Are you talking about cocaine, heroin, crack? Are you talking about marijuana? Are you talking about seeds or something? What exactly are you talking about?"

"Any drugs, period."

"Okay. Well, no. However, I'll give you an example … if we arrest somebody for a domestic or something, and they have a joint in their pocket, or half a joint, they smoked it then put it out, or just have seeds or something and we're charging them with the domestic, we just have them throw that in the trash, or we flush it down. We're not gonna charge them with a minor misdemeanor charge when we have them on a domestic. So, in that case, no, we don't report that. Now, if you're talking about cocaine or something, no, we put that in evidence. There's a difference."

The interview didn't last long, but it took them nearly a month to compile their report. On July 30, 2008 at a pre-disciplinary hearing, I was finally told what I was being charged with. When I saw the list, it made sense why they needed all that time. Added to the two charges I knew about were sixteen more—eighteen charges total.

Waves of shock, embarrassment, and anger washed over me as I read through the list.

I said the only thing I could say, "You've got to be kidding me!"

My experience in law and paralegal school and working as a union leader had taught me that the less I said the better. I understood all aspects of the procedures as opposed to being an officer whose experience is limited to the criminal side, where they're called into the courtroom and subpoenaed to testify. I knew how everything worked, how long things took, and what to expect. I knew to be patient, that there was a lot of procedural stuff that had to happen before the day of reckoning. And the one thing I knew best was not to show my hand early. I knew that it would behoove me to be quiet and patient, and just weather the storm until it was my day. Had I not had the experiences I'd had, I would've tried to exonerate myself on day one. It also helped that I'd fought this opponent before.

Unlike when I'd left college and hadn't taken advantage of the support available to me, I turned to the union for help.

I knew McGuire would go as far as he needed to go to get rid of me, so I wasn't surprised when I got the call from my union attorney, Joe Hegedus.

"Alright, Clayton. This is what they're gonna do … McGuire is going to send this to Diane Lind with his recommendation. He's a jerk. You know that. Like we've talked about, the next stage is probably going to be notification of termination. We'll file an appeal, but I just want you to be prepared for what's about to happen. It's one thing to talk about the possibility of it happening. It's another to talk about the eventuality of it happening. Got me?"

"Yeah. I got it." My analytical brain had processed it and got it, but the rest of me would take a while to catch up.

Unbeknownst to Joe, I'd already started working on Plan B. I had thought about my dad and how he always looked at all the options, and I added up my monthly bills for the next eight months. I could walk away and get another full-time job, or I could stick around and find a way to get back what I wanted. I knew exactly how much money I needed to buy the time I needed and added a buffer to cover anything I couldn't see coming. I'd also started substitute teaching in the Fostoria City Schools: elementary, middle, and high school.

A few days later, on my daughter's birthday, the phone rang.

It was Joe.

"McGuire submitted his findings to Diane Lind on the first. They've scheduled a date for your disciplinary hearing."

On a hot, muggy August day with the loan approved and the money in my bank account, Joe and I stepped into Lind's office. Sure enough, McGuire had submitted his report and told her that there was enough evidence to sustain sixteen of the eighteen charges against me. He'd recommended that I be fired.

"Hi, Clayton. Joe," she said in the same soft-spoken voice I'd heard since I was a kid. She motioned us to sit. Mrs. Lind as I'd called her back then had lived a couple of streets over from me when I was a kid, and I'd been her paperboy. I knew her family, her kids.

"Hey, Diane," I said as we sat down. "Firstly, I don't think you're qualified to handle this. I'm not trying to put you down or anything. I just don't think you're the right person to do this, and I'm not sure you have all the correct information or full picture."

There was no animosity, but none of us was comfortable.

She'd been working as the mayor's secretary, but the city had her fill in as the safety service director while they looked for someone to permanently fill the role. They'd let this fall on her because she was acting safety service director.

"I can understand how you feel, and I'm sorry to be the one sitting opposite you today, but this is what I have to do."

She'd laid a copy of the sixteen charges against me and the findings for Joe and me to look at while she read them and stated her—McGuire's—decision. My mind and body felt like they were in a million places at once. I saw the faces of my dad, my mom, my daughters, Pam, my students, my fellow officers, my friends, and the many faces of the kids I coached and their parents. I was glad they couldn't hear what I was hearing.

- Unauthorized release of confidential information

- Misuse of information without authorization

- Wanton or willful neglect of duties

- Dereliction of duties

- Intimidating or interfering with other employees

- Conduct violating common decency including sexual harassment

- Dishonest[y]/making false statement

- Giving false testimony during the investigation of a complaint

- Making false claims in an attempt to obtain a city benefit

- Creating a hostile work environment including sexual harassment

- Willful disregard of city rules, regulations, policies, or procedures

- Making or publishing false, vicious or malicious statements about employees or city operation

- Conduct unbecoming

- Unsatisfactory work or failure to maintain required standard of performance

- Willful failure to make required reports

- Disobeying department rules, policies, and procedures

On August 6, 2008, the city of Fostoria fired the first black police officer it had hired.

CHAPTER 10

GUILTY UNTIL PROVEN INNOCENT

*F*rom the beginning of the process, Pam was involved on a daily basis. As I became aware of each new thing, we were on the phone or together in person talking about it. She was my sounding board, my anger management coach, and most of all my rock, my support, my encouragement, and my energy. She was a big reason I was able to keep going forward. From day one, she told me to walk with my head up. She reminded me that I had nothing to be ashamed of, that I'd done nothing wrong, and that in time, others would know that as well.

Pam wasn't ashamed of me. She was proud of me. I couldn't have asked for anything more than what she gave me.

But before official word got out, there were three things I needed to do.

When I knocked on his door, Fostoria High School's football coach, Tom Grine, answered and invited me in. This was something I wanted to do in person, but that didn't make it easy to say. I hesitated before saying, "For

totally bogus reasons, I was let go from the police force ...
I wanted to come here to tell you in person that I'm
resigning from my coaching position, and—"

"Absolutely not!"

"But—"

"No, you're not, Clayton. As far as I'm concerned, that
has nothing to do with this football program or this school.
You know, that's McGuire's thing. He's doing that, but
I know who you are ... your character, Clayton. I know
that you're an asset to these young men on this team."

My chest was tight, and I was fighting back emotion.
I just stared through him and nodded.

"I'm not accepting your resignation. Call Tim and
see what he says, but I'm not doing this. You have my
full support."

I went home and called Tim Murray, the athletic director, who echoed Grine's sentiment. One Friday night not
long after I told them, I was on the field coaching players
during a warmup before a game, when Murray approached
me. "Hey, get your head up. Look at me," he said. As he
stared into my eyes, his words of encouragement, support,
and love penetrated my heart. Both he and Grine were
the two crutches I needed to hold me up while I was out
there. I didn't want to let either of them down. My stress
level went down slightly, but the hardest conversations
were ahead of me.

* * *

Just as I was finishing up in the weight room I have in the
back room of my house, my mom came in.

"Hi, sweetie. How ya doin'?" she said.

Seeing her and hearing her voice was all it took to bring tears to my eyes, and the weight I felt was far heavier than anything I'd just lifted.

"Mommy, I need to tell you something." I wiped the bench with the towel in my hand and motioned for her to sit.

She squinted her eyes and asked, "What did they say?"

"They let me go …"

"They did what!?" She raised her body as if she was going to stand. It was like she wasn't looking at Clayton the man. She was looking at her little boy, whom she'd encouraged to become a police officer in the first place. She let me know exactly how she felt about the mayor, the chief, and anybody else who'd had a hand in my dismissal.

I was fighting hard, holding back the tears as her emotions rose and she started crying. I tried not to look at her because I knew if I made eye contact, I'd start crying too.

"Hey, things are gonna be fine," I said.

"I wish Daddy was here," she said. Tears streamed down her face. I could barely keep myself together.

"I'm gonna be fine," I said. I was trying to reassure us both that I was tougher and stronger than this, and that they would need more than this to take me down.

She was dealing with enough. Her heart was failing, and, in fact, in the months that followed, she had heart surgery, and I took care of her.

Watching my mom suffer for and with me almost broke my heart. Telling her what had happened was the hardest thing I'd had to do; I was her baby boy. She loved me unconditionally, in a way parents are expected to love and support their kids. What I had to do next, the people I had to see next, I wondered what they would say, what they would do.

Pam's parents, Larry and Luci, had always been nice to me, but I knew that people were going to talk. They were going to hear things. And we tend to believe what we hear unless we hear another side of the story. But I wasn't going to be able to tell that other side, to defend myself. I needed to stay quiet, but sometimes people see silence as an admission of guilt. I couldn't let Pam's parents get blindsided. Telling them in person what was going on was my way of showing respect, but just like with coach Grine, sitting in their living room face-to-face was tough.

Pam and I sat across from them, and I told them about the list of charges. Then I said, "I'm innocent of everything. I would never do anything to hurt your daughter, and I just want to tell you both about what's going on because obviously she's connected to me, so people are gonna talk to you about it and say stuff like, 'Your daughter's with this kind of guy?' and I just want you guys to know that this—the guy sitting in front of you, not the guy people are saying I am—is who I am."

They didn't flinch. Their demeanor was open.

I went on. "I can't say a whole lot, but if you have any questions, I'll do my best to answer."

They had a few but nothing deep.

When Pam and I got up to leave, both of her parents hugged me.

"Clayton," Larry said. "If you need anything, you let us know."

From day one, I had the unwavering support of the people closest to me. I was going to need it.

* * *

I'd known something like this was coming, but when I unfolded the paper a few days after my meeting with Lind, I wasn't prepared to be front page news:

> It was a not-so-sweet 16 that led to the recent termination of Fostoria Police Sgt. Clayton Moore.
>
> According to Moore's personnel file...18 allegations were made against him.
>
> Two of the allegations were found to be unsubstantiated, but the other 16 were considered intolerable, according to a memo from Police Chief John McGuire to Interim Safety Director Diane Lind.
>
> Allegations range from making a claim to obtain a benefit from a false overtime slip to two counts of "wanton and willful neglect of duties..."[1]

They say that anger is a secondary emotion. Whether it is or isn't I can't say. What I can say is, in those first few hours after reading the article, anger was all I felt. When it started to fade, fear and shame took over. I became a prisoner in my own house. I was too ashamed to go out. I felt like a victim because I knew what was in the papers. Clayton Moore. The Lone Ranger. No gun. No badge. No hero. I imagined what people were thinking and saying, and I just didn't want to socialize with anyone. I didn't want to face them. It was hard for me to coach at the time, but coaching was one of the only things that got me out of the house.

One Friday night at a football game, the things I imagined people were saying were confirmed. I stuck pretty close to the coaches and players and tried not to look at the people who came to watch the game, but on that night, I heard people talking low behind me. My mind started racing, wondering if they were talking about me or if they were just talking like people do about this and that and I was just being paranoid. Then one of the guys raised his voice and spat out, "You used to be a cop. You ain't no cop no more." It felt like I'd been punched in the back of the head, and I just had to take it. I could punch back with, "Yeah, well it's easy to judge when you only have one version of the story and that version is being told by the people in power. If you could think for yourself, you might ask questions rather than throw out trash like that." Of course, even if he had asked questions, I wouldn't have been able to answer.

I wonder how Muhammad Ali felt knowing he was right but suffered the consequences of his decision not to submit to the draft. He was a fighter, a literal come-out-swinging, hit-your-opponent-in-the-face fighter, but he chose not to come out swinging. He submitted to the process and made his case within the system so he could change the system. I wish I could say that I felt noble at the time, but I didn't. What I did do was stay quiet and submit to the process.

What I couldn't say to the obtuse dude in the bleachers that night and every other casual observer was documented in the union's grievance filed on my behalf about the time the story hit the front page of our local paper. The union grievance addressed the charges leveled against me, focusing on the city's misuse of due process and employment law.

Essentially, the city ignored the principles of just cause. Just cause requires an employer to act in a reasonable and fair manner, and not to act in any manner that is arbitrary, capricious or discriminatory. In addition, an employer is obligated to use progressive discipline—that is, which is not excessive and is designed to correct rather than punish. That didn't happen in my case.

A number of my contractual due process rights were violated, e.g., failure to provide the alleged charges in writing, and scheduling a pre-disciplinary conference no sooner than 48 hours from the time of notice. I was not informed as to the nature of any investigation prior to my questioning. I was told only that the scope of the interview was to determine facts and statements concerning alleged violations of the policy, procedures, rules, regulations and directives of the Fostoria Police Department. This is significant in that McGuire then tried to claim that my answers to overbroad questions asked by Marx, based on vague allegations, were not complete or comprehensive enough. The city used the lack of specificity of its allegations to charge that I was untruthful or that my answers changed over time. It acknowledged that as I became aware of the specific incidents alleged, including the identity of persons involved and dates and times that matters were alleged to have occurred, I then offered further information concerning my actions. However, my attempt to provide accurate and comprehensive information by supplementing and/or clarifying the record as charges were stated to me only gave them more ammunition.

As to the specific charges, I and my union representative were prepared to demonstrate that the city had overstepped its bounds in their zeal to manufacture a case against me. Some examples:

- I was accused of making a false claim or misrepresentation regarding overtime. The city failed to prove this. I had worked the midnight shift for more than 20 years; any work during the day shift was overtime for me, and the approval of overtime by my supervisor led me to believe that I was entitled to overtime for my time spent pursuant to the order to report to Marx's office. I was never paid the overtime. After the union's attorney explained that I was not entitled to it, I dropped the matter.

- The City accused me of "misuse [of] confidential information" when I requested an employee to run a license plate. Patrick Brooks, a captain, acknowledged that I had a legitimate reason to run the plate, but he did not feel that it was appropriate because I was on administrative leave. I was never informed that I had no privileges as a police officer while on administrative leave.

- I did not threaten, coerce, or interfere with the Law Director Hoover during our conversation in November 2007, and no question was even raised about it until March 2008. The conversation had been initiated by Hoover and took place while I was off-duty and in civilian clothes. Hoover asked if I had any issues with the prosecutor's office. I simply told him not to become too close to McGuire. It was an honest answer to a city official's question.

- In no way did I become "improperly involved in the investigation" of the case concerning my brother, Damon Moore. In fact, I made it a point to stay as far away as possible from my brother's case: I did not review any of the reports of the incident or exert any supervisory authority in the case; I left the station when Damon was interviewed; and I did not give any input regarding the charge that would be filed. The city did not call Officer Cory Echelberry, who investigated the incident, to testify, and Marx testified that Echelberry did not disclose information sufficient to establish that I interfered in his investigation.

- Nor was I "out of line" in contacting Carol Reffner about Damon's bond. She later expressed regret for having created the impression that she would recommend an own-recognizance bond. I was not trying to influence the decision regarding the bond; I only wanted to be able to inform family members about the amount of cash they might need.

- I did not threaten, intimidate, coerce, or interfere with Hoover during our conversation at the Seneca county courthouse. Hoover's version of the events, solicited by McGuire two months after the conversation took place, was not corroborated by the one objective third-party witness. The setting, scope and tone of that conversation was exactly as I described it earlier in this book.

- I never deviated from standard policy or practice by taking narcotics from a suspect. The two original allegations related to this had occurred eight years prior; neither of the individuals involved in those events were interviewed. I told Marx that under prior police chiefs, it was an accepted practice to take small amounts of marijuana or marijuana seeds from suspects and to destroy them; this was confirmed by Brooks. The city subsequently admitted that it had no proof, and those charges were subsequently dropped.

- In regard to the claim that I made "false, vicious, or malicious statements" about other employees, my brief conversation with Nesbitt in a city parking lot simply conveyed that things in the department were "difficult" for me.

- I never engaged in the improper and unauthorized release of confidential information regarding Joanne Kitzler, an administrative assistant in the department. I did not state that she had been charged with forgery or other felony. My comments about Kitzler were made in private to Nesbitt, and any reference to a crime were based on the department's rumor mill. I never approached Kitzler regarding her alleged criminal history or degraded her to her face, or said anything about her to anyone but Nesbitt. Nesbitt relayed my comments to Kitzler in private; Kitzler later admitted that she wanted Holly Cassidy, a coworker, to hear what Nesbitt had told her. I did not refer to Kitzler as a "bimbo."

- I did not make and then fail to report a traffic stop or operate my police vehicle in an unsafe manner in December 2007. I was unaware of these charges until the pre-disciplinary conference on July 30, 2008. In the incident described, I did not initiate a traffic stop; rather, I stopped behind Gayle Martin, a fellow member of my church's finance committee, who recognized me and pulled over to talk. Because it was 2:00 a.m., I followed her to a bank where she had business to conduct.

- Contrary to the City's assertion, I did not fail to file a report about a fight and lockdown at Fostoria High School. There was a verbal altercation between a female student and two male students but there was no physical altercation. By the time I arrived, the matter had de-escalated, no police assistance was required, and I asked the dispatcher to close out the case (a common practice in our department until the procedure was discontinued in May or June of 2008). I was stationed at the school for the remainder of that day, and I did not have a chance to file a report because I was placed on administrative leave the following day. A subsequent investigation confirmed that the school had indicated the incident would be handled internally and that no further police assistance was needed.

- After the city submitted allegations made by Stephanie Dickson, which they characterized as sexual harassment, they failed to call Dickson as a witness, which due process requires. Dickson had refused to be interviewed as part of the internal investigation. She never claimed that my conduct amounted to "unwelcome sexual advances, requests for sexual favors, or other verbal or physical contact of a sexual nature" or that my conduct created an "offensive, hostile, or intimidating work environment" or prevented her from "effectively performing the duties of her position." She only alleged that she felt "uncomfortable" by our one conversation the night of the drug raid. Dickson did not file charges against me and the METRICH board decided not to further investigate the allegations.

The union submitted its grievance on my behalf, asking the arbitrator to direct the city to make the grievant whole—i.e., to rescind all of the disciplinary action against me, and to remove all evidence of the discipline from any employment-related file.[2] Then we waited for the arbitrator's decision.

* * *

Hearing people talk behind my back and say ignorant things reminded me of Calvin and all the people I'd arrested throughout my career. The American judicial system is romanticized. In principle the accused are innocent until proven guilty. It sounds good, but in practice—especially in smaller towns and cities where everyone knows everything—you're often considered guilty until proven innocent. The powers-that-be control the narrative, and defendants are tried in the court of public opinion. Facts don't matter. Perception is reality. And for some who prove themselves not guilty, it's still not like they've proved themselves innocent. They're often seen as having gotten off, or having gotten away with it.

For too many, even when they "win," the damage has been done.

I went home and cried for the I don't know how many-th time. I walked around my house and asked the same question I'd asked since this whole thing started,

"Why, God? Why me?" I couldn't eat. I couldn't sleep. I'd start crying out of the blue, and all I could think at those times was *What did I do to deserve this? Why has God abandoned me?*

* * *

Certain numbers in the Bible are very significant; one of them is 3. One afternoon while driving home, the first of three things happened.

I was about half a block from my house when I started crying. I said out loud, "God, why are you putting me through this?" As soon as I said that, a Hispanic man in a truck pulled up beside me. He pulled up right beside my car, looked at me, and rolled the window down. I rolled my window down, trying to fight the tears back. He put his right arm on top of the passenger side bench seat and leaned across the passenger seat toward me.

"Hey, brother," he said. "How you doing?"

"Fine," I said.

"I just want you to know one thing," he said. "You're gonna fight this, aren't you? You're not gonna just let—"

His words had an energy.

"Yeah. I'm gonna fight," I called back.

"Good. We got your back," he said as he straightened back up and looked forward. Then he turned again and said, "We're supporting you." And then he drove off.

I said, "Okay" to nobody and everybody.

Later, I found out that he's a minister at a church located around the corner from where I live. At the time, I had no idea who he was. I still don't know his name, but I see him every once in a while. When I do, I always wave to him and say "hi."

Two or three days later, I was in my house once again walking around and crying, saying the same thing, "God, why are you putting me through this? What did I do wrong?" Within thirty seconds, my phone rang. On the other end of the line was a lady that worked with my mom. She said, "Hey, how you doing?"

"Fine," I lied.

She said, "Hey, listen. I was just thinking about you. I just wanted to sing you a song."

She sang me a song that she'd sung at church.

I listened and wept.

When she finished, she said, "I'm thinking about you and praying for you, Clayton."

All I could say was, "Okay."

That was it. She sang, said she was praying for me, then hung up.

With nothing but time on my hands and no desire to go out, I worked out more than usual. It calmed my body but not my mind. I still couldn't get past seeing myself as a victim. I kept asking God, *Why?*

One day during a why-and-weightlifting session, I heard the doorbell. It was my mom.

"How you doing, son?"

I faked like I wasn't in a deep funk and said my latest catch phrase, "Fine."

"Well, I came over to tell you that the church people want to have a benefit barbeque rib and chicken dinner. All the proceeds will go to you."

I was speechless. I'd been feeling hurt, ashamed, and angry, strong emotions, but in that moment, I was tremendously humbled and felt so appreciated and appreciative. As much as I already loved my church family, I fell in love with them even more. I later found out that the event was spearheaded by the late Mr. John C. Meekins. He put the idea in front of Pastor T.A. Smith, and Meekins, the pastor, and Ernest "Champ" Tucker put the ball in motion. The men of the church purchased all the meat, and the women of the church made the side dishes. At the end of the event, I received over $800. That was my church family telling me that they loved and supported me. More importantly, I knew it was God's way of saying, "I'm here. I'm here for you, and I'm not gonna let you go. Just bear with me. Let me do my work. I'm using you for something bigger than you."

At that moment, an energy went through my body. It was like I'd been carrying 5,000 pounds on my shoulders, and someone took it off. Later that night at home in the quiet house, I looked up and smiled and said, "Okay, God. I get it. Thank you."

That was a gift, and I was able to give back during the time when my mom had her triple bypass surgery. I wasn't working, so I was there for her every morning and afternoon. I was able to reassure myself that things happen for a reason. I was there for my mom to help her get back to normal, to make sure she did her exercises. My job was to get her walking up and down the street and help her with her breathing treatment. During that time, I saw myself as her physical trainer.

After the fundraiser, Mom and I had a talk about everything that was going on and how I was coping. "Mommy, listen. I'm gonna be fine. I'm different, you know."

She looked at me and said, "What do you mean?"

"Different. I'm different." I paused. "I knew this when I was a child … I'm not special. I'm no better than anybody else, but I'm different. There's something different about me, and I've always known that. This isn't even about me ... This has nothing to do with me. It's about something else, somebody else, and God's just using me as a vessel. Of all the people He could have chosen, He chose me, you know? It's just a blessing, and I'm not going to let Him down. I'm going to be strong. I just need to do His work." After that, I had so much peace. Even though my appeal had been denied, and it was true, I wasn't no cop no more (at least not on paper), I was going to be okay.

From that time on when I looked in the mirror, I saw myself clearly. I saw the boy who wanted to make his parents proud, the kid who said "no" in the face of pressure to go along with the crowd, the man who chased his dreams even when his chances of grasping them got smaller and smaller, a man who stuck around and took care of his family, who loved his kids, and stepped up to be a leader and example to kids in his community. I saw the immature cop with big hair and a big mouth, the cop I'd grown to be, and the cop I still wanted to be. And I heard what God was saying to me through His apostle Paul in his letter to the Hebrews: "... let us lay aside every weight ... and let us run with endurance the race that is set before us ..."[3]

I appealed the city's decision, which meant another round of hearings and procedures. (For those interested in the highly detailed "Union Statement of the Case and of the Pertinent Facts" crafted by union attorney Joe Hegedus, which was submitted on January 26, 2009, please see Appendix.)

After my firing and during the arbitration process, Pat Brooks took and passed the captain's test. Even if I did get my job back, I would forever be his subordinate.

* * *

On March 9, 2009, I was in my car driving to Toledo with my daughter Erica when my cell phone rang. It was Joe.

Tears were running down my face when I hung up.

"Daddy, what's wrong?"

"Nothing babe," I said. "We won. We just won."

I didn't wait until I got home to tell Pam. I called her immediately. Her reaction was as strong as Joe's had been. Both had been incensed by the mockery of due process and targeted assault on an innocent officer. This was a win for all of us.

Soon after I received a copy of the written verdict. The first eleven words say it all:

> *This case concerns an egregious attempt by the city of Fostoria (the "city") to impose the industrial death penalty on a twenty-three-year employee after a sham investigation and without adequate substantive evidence of wrongdoing.*
>
> *The weakness of the city's case is laid bare by the number of allegations that are either untimely, lacking in specificity and/or wholly unsupported in the actual record evidence.*
>
> *Moreover, undeterred by its total lack of evidence in support of its enumerated bogus allegations against the grievant—Clayton Moore ("Moore"), the city then recklessly accuses Moore generally of dishonesty, despite its inability to specify with any particularity where or when any of these falsehoods purportedly occurred. Additionally, the city plainly admits that Moore was never given a detailed list, after the investigation, of the distinct written charges, until during his pre-disciplinary conference. Yet, the city wants this arbiter to believe that Moore was less than forthcoming during an "investigation" where he*

was forced to glean his alleged wrongdoing from vaguely worded questions covering broad topics over the period of his entire career.

The foregoing clearly illustrates that there was no just cause for the discipline in this case and that principles of progressive discipline were completely ignored.

Consequently, the grievant should be reinstated with full back pay and seniority, and any benefits lost as a result of his improper termination should be restored. Additionally, all documents related to the discipline in this case should be removed from Moore's personnel file.[4]

* * *

His statement still hangs in my office, printed and mounted in an attention-grabbing gold frame, a reminder and part of the permanent record of who I am and what kind of police officer I was.

Putting on my uniform and pulling on my hat on my first day back at work was one of the most satisfying experiences of my life. I'd done the work. I'd earned my place.

CHAPTER 11

CROSSING THE LINE

I had my job back and thanks to the arbiter's statement, I was insulated from any more McGuire-related drama. And through a series of events, he removed himself from the equation—by way of a worker's compensation claim that led to him taking some nine months off. In his absence, Pat Brooks served as acting chief. When McGuire's contract came up for renewal, the city chose not to offer him another contract.

Keith Lorano, Fostoria's fire chief, was tapped for the job because he held both licenses—fire and police chief. Many of us thought that the city was trying to save money by not hiring a separate police chief and instead giving Lorano a pay raise and assigning him to both roles. It sounds crazy under normal circumstances, but knowing what we knew about the city of Fostoria, it wouldn't have surprised us to learn that that was the reasoning behind the move.

Regardless, Lorano is highly qualified and a good guy. Working under his command was a pleasure. When Lorano took over as chief of police, Pat Brooks resumed his role as captain.

Not long after being reinstated, I ran against Pat for president of the command officers bargaining unit of the OPBA. Brooks was pissed, but in my mind, there was a conflict of interest. As the captain, he was the one responsible for filing charges against officers below him. The role of the union and the leaders representing them is to educate officers about their contractual rights and help them navigate the process if they are ever charged with a discipline-worthy offense.

"Pat, you cannot be our union president and captain when you are the one capable of handing down disciplinary action against other officers. That's a conflict of interest, you know?"

He didn't like that, but I went on. "Here's the thing. Let's say you were to write me up for something. You're a captain. I'm a sergeant. If you were to write me up for something and I have to be represented, I would have to go to you to represent me. But you were the one who wrote me up. It doesn't make any sense."

Our peers agreed. I was elected as president of the command unit and was a contract phenom. My sports law classes, sports agent training, paralegal degree, and firsthand experience of being wrongly accused and finally vindicated gave me a perspective no one else had. I helped negotiate excellent contracts on behalf of our members and supported officers through difficult times.

My own difficult times seemed to be behind me. Pam and I got married, and we were watching our kids grow up and go out into the world to pursue their own goals and dreams. One of those had the same dream I'd had at his age, but, like my brother, had gotten to see it become a reality.

In the fall of 2015, Pam and I loaded up our car and drove toward Green Bay, Wisconsin to watch her son Micah play as a starter with the Green Bay Packers. While driving across Indiana, I looked in my rearview mirror and saw the flashing lights of a highway patrol car behind me and coming up fast.

I pulled to the side of the road and prepared for the drill I'd been through hundreds of times but always on the other side of the car door. The exchange started like it usually does, "Do you know how fast you were going back there…"

"Hey, officer," I said and continued in a cooperative and respectful manner. The trooper treated me like I was beneath him. His gestures, his look, his mannerism, and tone reminded me of the slave master mentality as if he were looking at me and calling me a "boy" without saying it. When he asked for my license and registration, I wanted to get out there and whoop his ass.

"My I.D. is in my glove box. There's also a weapon in there."

He leaned toward me. "Why do you have a weapon?"

"It's my off-duty weapon."

"Let me see your I.D."

Instead, I handed him my badge and I.D. together.

He looked in at me and adjusted his belt and said, "Are you an officer?"

"Yes," is all I said. I could see Pam in my peripheral vision. Her body language said everything I wanted to say.

"Are you part-time?"

"No, our department don't have no part-time officers."

When he went back to his vehicle to run my info, Pam turned in her seat. She was more pissed than I was.

I said, "Pam don't worry … Don't say nothing, don't say nothing. Let's just get this over with and get out of here."

When the officer came back and handed me the citation, I just took it and left.

When I hear people say that there's not racial bias, that black men and other men of color are getting pulled over and arrested more because they're doing more of the crime, I can tell them that I've experienced bias as a police officer. They cannot tell me that this doesn't happen or that the few times it does happen it gets blown out of proportion. When they say there's no institutional racism, I can only say that they don't get it. They don't live my life, or the lives of all black men and women.

I'm not saying to swing the pendulum the other way and not pull someone over or arrest them if they're black. No. Like Detective Baretta on the cop show said a long time ago, "If you do the crime, you do the time." But if you haven't done a crime, or if the crime like a minor speeding infraction doesn't warrant an authoritarian response, back it down a notch. Treat everybody the same. Period.

A few months after that incident, Pam, my white wife, and I were sitting on the couch in our living room when she turned to me and said something that brought tears to my eyes. "You know what, Clayton?"

"What, Babe?"

"When I get pulled over by police officers and I'm by myself, I'm not afraid at all. I'm only afraid when I'm with you or Micah, and you get pulled over."

Her words hit me like a ton of bricks. It was her tone, her look, and the pain with which she expressed it.

Although I have my suspicions based on things I've heard the people involved say, I can't say for sure whether the reputational and financial threat I faced was the result of racial bias. What I can say is that the physical threats I face as a black man become all too real when I slide behind the wheel of my car or do any number of other things white people never think twice about. At the end of the day, all I want is what everyone else wants, to be there for and to take care of my family.

In the spring of 2018, I was trying to get some paperwork filed for one of Pam's sons, my stepson. He'd been having some issues and we were caring for him full-time. I needed to get some information for a document I needed to fill out on his behalf and needed to make sure the license plate I was looking at was the correct one for his vehicle. So, like I'd done hundreds of times before, I called the recorded dispatch line.

"Hey, it's Clayton. Can you run my stepson's plate through LEADS for me? I need to do some insurance paperwork, and he's not around to confirm the info I need."

"Yep, no problem. Give me just a second."

The dispatcher ran the plate and confirmed that it was the correct one. I thanked him and got off the phone.

LEADS stands for Law Enforcement Data System. The only acceptable use of the system is for work purposes. You can't use it to stalk someone or get confidential information to use against someone, but "work purposes" is a general term. Officers use LEADS all the time to serve citizens just as I had tried to do for Mr. Parker.

Running a plate is not a big deal. Except it is a big deal when the wrong person hears about you doing something and is looking to screw you over. Despite the chief telling him to chill out, Captain Brooks went behind the chief, got the information through LEADS, took it over to the prosecutor in Tiffin, and once again, my attorney and I had to go in and figure out what was going on. When we showed up for the meeting we were told about the alleged violation, and I was asked, "How close are you to retirement? What's your retirement date?" I told them and they gave me until the end of August to retire.

If the concern was for the law and to protect the department from an erosion of public trust, the dispatcher who with full knowledge of who I am and the purpose of the request ran the plate should have faced disciplinary action too. He did not.

It was clear. This wasn't about rules or justice. It wasn't about the dispatcher. It was about me. It struck me then as it does now that if there is a war on cops, as some would have us believe, it is a civil one.

I could have stayed and fought again, but when I ran the numbers this time, retiring early would only cost me $30,000. This time, it seemed God was telling me it was time to continue my work—His work—somewhere else. My race was over, and I was fine with that.

In a somewhat poetic twist, one daughter's birthday marked the penultimate chapter in my career as a law enforcement officer, and my other daughter's birthday marked the closing page of that book. On her birthday in July of 2018, I walked out the doors of the Fostoria Police Department, took off my uniform and transitioned from Clayton the cop to Clayton the citizen.

* * *

For almost all my life all I've wanted is to make my parents proud, to love and be loved and take care of my family, and to be someone other people can look up to. My only fear has been that of not living up to who I want to be. Like every athlete, every runner, I've never been afraid of taking a step. I just want to make sure I take good steps and take enough steps and do what I need to do to play my part.

I live in Fostoria, Ohio. I probably always will.

I serve in Fostoria, Ohio. Unless I move elsewhere, I always will.

I stand shoulder to shoulder with Calvin who in spite of a few mistakes has become a pillar of our community.

I say "hi" to Diane Lind when I see her. She says "hi" to me. Our relationship is not defined by one bad day or one moment in time.

Our pasts do not define us. What others say does not define us. Only how we react to others and treat others matters, and what we tell ourselves matters, and what we do moving forward matters.

Shortly after deciding to write this book, I was pulling in my trash bins when a woman walked by on the sidewalk.

"Hey, Clayton," she called out.

"How you doing?" I asked her.

"I've been clean for thirty days now," she said.

"Ay, awesome," I said. "Keep it up!"

I didn't recognize her, don't know who she is, but God knows. And God's working on her, and apparently, I was part of the work.

And this book is God still working on me and my way of continuing to live out my identity as a servant and protector.

AFTERWORD:
BLACK LIVES MATTER*

As a black man, I experience racial discrimination. As a cop, I came to understand the unpredictable nature of humans and the dangers police officers face every day. As a black cop, I experienced what black men and those who love them experience all too often when they are pulled over by an officer of the law. When people talk about the Black Lives Matter movement being a war on cops or that it somehow elevates black lives over the lives of others, and when they criticize professional athletes for exercising their right to free speech and tell them to stick to what they're good at and suggest that it is somehow inappropriate for athletes to use their platforms to make political statements, I must say something.

I believe that as a black cop and the father-in-law of a biracial (non-white) NFL player, I can offer a nuanced view that brings people with different perspectives together to discuss things in a rational and respectful manner.

For me, this movement says Black Lives Matter *too*.

DIFFERENT RULES FOR DIFFERENT GROUPS

One of the biggest problems I have with objections to the Black Lives Matter movement is that there is one set of standards for one group, another set of standards for the other.

White, conservative celebrities such as Charlton Heston and Clint Eastwood are allowed close ties to and even leadership positions in the National Rifle Association (NRA). They are permitted by those opposed to the Black Lives Matter movement to be vocal supporters of an organization often called to account by supporters of the Black Lives Matter movement. The NRA, according to PolitiFact, a non-partisan fact-checking website, "has spent $203.2 million on political activities since 1998."[1] The Black Lives Matter movement is a largely grassroots movement that calls for equality not just in principle *under* the law but exercised *by* the law. Supporters of the Black Lives Matter Movement want accountability, a very American value.

While the predominantly white and conservative group is permitted to use their platform in support of the Second Amendment, the predominately people of color and liberal group is not permitted to use theirs to exercise and support the First Amendment.

We should at least all play by the same rules as they do in professional sports. But even there the rules do not apply equally to everyone.

When taxpayers pay for military flyovers before sporting events, when pre-game ceremonies include the Pledge of Allegiance and singing of the national anthem, we make sports political. When we exclude from media coverage or penalize players who silently and peacefully protest by kneeling during the national anthem, we come dangerously close to using sports as propaganda.

It seems disingenuous—and insults the intelligence of listeners—for one group to criticize another for the very thing it's doing.

I want us to focus on the core message of the Black Lives Matter movement and come together not to protect ourselves from one another but to engage in ways that remove the need to bear arms for protection from one another—cops from men of color and men of color from cops. To do that, it's important to understand that the Black Lives Matter movement is not the Black Liberation Army. The Black Liberation Army grew out of the Civil Rights movement but went beyond a demand for equal rights under the law and in practice by means of peaceful demonstration and intellectual engagement to supporting violence as a means to a political end.

With few exceptions, no one who claims to be part of the Black Lives Matter movement is calling for a war on police or to take up arms against whites or any other group of people. The Black Lives Matter movement has nothing to do with taking up arms. People within the Black Lives Matter movement are basically saying, "Quit killing our black youth. Our lives matter too." That's all they're saying. We want justice for our young, black Americans who seem to be killed at a higher rate than anybody else. Now, I'm not sure if it's true that young, black men are being killed at a higher rate. We need to look at all the data, to have access to all the data. What's easy to see is that they have gotten more notoriety because for the most part it's been a white officer killing an unarmed black man. And if it is, if one racial group is doing more killing of another racial group than another, we must ask ourselves why.

That's why people are saying, "Hey. Can you stop this? Can you stop what we feel is unjust killings of our people? Our lives matter too. They matter just as much as the brown lives matter. They matter just like the white lives matter. Will you please stop this?"

No one is looking for a war. We're looking for solutions.

There's no one in the Black Lives Matter movement who's saying, "Let's go shoot police officers." They want the protection of police officers. They understand protection. They understand that there are a lot of African American police officers. Some of their family members are police officers. Come on. Let's be real and focus on the real problems and real solutions because at the end of the day, every life matters.

With that in mind, here are what I see as practical and relatively easy changes we can make to the system and within each of our own lives, so we can all be part of the solution and be insulated from violence.

POLICE FORCES THAT REFLECT THE COMMUNITY

Police forces are becoming more diverse, but in many areas law enforcement is still predominantly white even when the community it serves is far more diverse. This creates an obvious line between groups, and doesn't give communities of color a sense that they're seen as equal and integral to the overall community. I didn't go through a lot of the struggles that other African Americans have gone through, but look at how I responded to my mom: "I ain't trying to be no cop." So, if we want to see police that reflect the communities they serve we're really talking about changing the mentality on both sides.

It's unreasonable to think that we can diversify the police overnight. That's a long-term project. But while we're working toward that, we can do better educating officers about the customs and cultures of the people they're tasked with serving. And it's not just white officers who need this. All of us have unconscious biases. Even officers of color become enculturated with the idea that people of color are more likely to commit crimes because they're dealing with the higher percentage of people of color being arrested, but this is only part of the story.

The other part is hard to tell because it requires data about the number of crimes actually being committed and by whom. As I mentioned before, money buys space—privacy. Cybercrimes, abuse, and other "white collar" crimes are happening all around us but can go undetected for years. Physical crimes such as robbery, murder, and drug sales that happen in high-population areas are far easier to detect. There's also physical and other relatively easy to obtain evidence. Naturally those crimes will be solved at a higher rate and unlike other crimes that are seen as "victimless" or less interesting to the crime documentary-watching public, more attention will be paid to them. This attention makes us susceptible to causal reductionism, the phenomenon that what is focal is causal.

It is a fact that there are more men and women of color in the criminal justice system. What has not been established—because it would require full knowledge of all crimes being committed and a full profile of the perpetrators—is that people of color, blacks in particular, are committing more crimes, and therefore, are crying foul in an effort to deflect attention away from their misdeeds. But that notion persists even among law enforcement officers who operate—in theory—under the ethos of innocent until proven guilty.

Things That Make White People Uncomfortable, Super Bowl champion and three-time Pro Bowler Michael Bennett shares an experience he had with two officers of color in Las Vegas that demonstrates how this biased thinking even seems to infect non-white police officers.

After attending a sporting event at a casino in Las Vegas, Bennett was standing in the lobby people watching when all hell broke loose. According to Bennett, someone shouted, "Gunshots! Gun! Gun! Shots fired!" Police stormed in and commanded everyone to evacuate. Like every other reasonable human in the area, nobody had to tell him twice. He ran for his life. As he did, officers followed and tackled him. They pinned him to the ground, cuffed him, and with a gun to his head one of them said that if he moved, the officer would shoot him right then and there (I've scrubbed the obscenity used by the officer). He was manhandled into a squad car—without charge—and left there. After Googling him, the officers realized who he was and let the famous football player go. After going public, the police officer's union accused him of lying and demanded that the NFL investigate what they called his "false statements."

Bystander video showed exactly what had happened and that Bennett's statements accurately described the scene. For some reason that as of the publishing of Bennett's book had not come to light, the officers involved had inexplicably turned off their body cams. But Bennett's claims of racial profiling and bias were rebutted with the fact that because the officers involved are Hispanic, bias and profiling couldn't be the explanation.[2]

If Bennett's case were the only one of its kind, we could easily dismiss it as an outlier. It is not and we should not. We need to make a concerted effort to look at all the factors and see how the mismatch between the racial makeup of police departments and the people they serve factors into bias and police brutality. We need greater diversity in our police forces and better cultural awareness training.

BETTER CULTURAL AWARENESS TRAINING

We need more cultural diversity training to understand that discrimination in the criminal justice system is real; this is happening. We've got to quit trying to skate over it. It's real, and our political climate only makes it worse because when Donald Trump—the then President of the United States—vilifies elected officials of color and tells them to go back to the dirty, crime-infested areas they came from, implying and sometimes outright stating that they are corrupt and untrustworthy, it offends all of us and damages the country in untold ways.

BETTER MENTAL HEALTH SCREENING FOR LAW ENFORCEMENT CANDIDATES

What cultural awareness training won't help with is trigger-happy cops, the ones who join and stay on the force because they like power and the level of control and protection the badge gives them. When it comes to power-hungry, hero-complex cops, it's much easier to target marginalized groups such as people of color. To keep citizens and police officers safe, we must implement more stringent psychological screening because research shows that officers who share these traits are more likely to fire their weapons.

A Pew Institute survey showed the following: "To start, male officers, white officers, those working in larger cities and those who are military veterans are more likely than female officers, racial and ethnic minorities, those in smaller communities and non-veterans to have ever fired their service weapon while on duty."[3]

That shouldn't automatically disqualify anyone who falls into one of the groups that have higher rates of duty weapon use. That would be profiling of a different, and still unacceptable, kind. To avoid that and protect all our rights, we must put in place systems that accurately assess each of us on an individual level. Although not the only means, psychological screening helps to do that.

BODY CAMS AND BUDGET

Had I been wearing a body cam or at least a mic during our undercover investigation and had those tapes been archived, the sexual harassment charge related to the events of that night could easily have been investigated and dismissed, but I didn't have that protection. The reality is that many law enforcement agencies don't use them or their use is limited.[4] Just because an agency or department uses them doesn't mean that every officer has one, or uses it. In places where the biggest crime tends to be running a red light, requiring officers to wear body cameras would be a waste of resources. While it would go a long way in proving a civilian or officer's innocence and provide context when reviewing volatile situations, to equip every officer with the technology would be extremely expensive, and those expenses fall on taxpayers.

As I've said, I support the Black Lives Matter movement and the professional athletes who are taking a knee and speaking out against police brutality and unfair treatment of people of color. But we need more than talk. We need meaningful action. I'd like to see these guys and the NFL players union start equipping police officers in areas where there's a greater chance of an officer shooting a black or brown man or woman. By doing so, they'd be saying to black, white, and brown officers, "We appreciate what you're doing. We have your back. We want to help you." That's going to disarm anyone who claims that the Black Lives Matter movement is a war on cops or that if a person stands up against police brutality, they are as Sheriff David Clarke Jr. characterized them, a "cop hater."[5] And, it's going to go a long way in changing the mentality of white officers who feel vilified or seen as less than trustworthy just because of the color of *their* skin.

POLICE RESIDENCY: IN THE COMMUNITY AND OF THE COMMUNITY

In addition to properly screening would-be officers and eliminating those who demonstrate a tendency toward aggression and lack of empathy, we need to have officers, regardless of their ethnicity, living in the same communities in which they work because when officers live in the communities they work in, they naturally interact with community members while off duty. Community members can get to know officers on a personal level, not just an authority level. And, as I found in my career, it's helpful to see suspects not as "perps" but as so and so's daughter or son or mother or father. When we know and see each other like that, respect is a byproduct, and abuse of power is less likely to occur. And this bond, in some cases friendship, can smooth high-emotion professional interactions, keeping officers, suspects, and bystanders safer. But those relationships can't form if officers haven't grown up in the community or if they aren't willing or able to live there.

CIVILIANS WHO SERVE AND PROTECT

We the people must be active community members. We can do that by volunteering and promoting volunteerism. Business owners could give employees a set number of on-the-job hours per month to volunteer with youth organizations such as Big Brothers Big Sisters. Those who cannot afford that could set up some kind of acknowledgement or reward system for employees who use their personal time to serve others.

This would be especially powerful if African American, Hispanic, and officers from refugee families were interacting with kids. Kids need role models. I'm all for professional sports figures and titans of business as role models, but not everyone has the physical potential to be a professional athlete or interest and aptitude for entrepreneurship and corporate business. They especially need role models in occupations and places of interest to them.

When we help others, we feel empowered and respected. When we're always the ones being helped, it can be disempowering, like we are less than. We've got to change that.

* * *

If things are going to change, if we as citizens are going to have a positive impact, and if police officers are truly going to serve and protect, we must be humble. We've all got to look at ourselves and the mistakes we've made and forgive ourselves and move forward. We've got to let go of our labels and the labels we give others. We've got to open our eyes and see others for who they are and what they can be, get up and serve the adults in our communities and those who are coming up, and be a force for change. If we aren't willing to do that, I don't think we have a right to complain no matter which side of the argument we're on. It doesn't take a whole lot of effort to do something good, but it does take *some* effort.

I challenge you, reader, to decide what's most important to you and where you can make the most difference, find an opportunity to serve that fits that, and go out there and do your thing. Do something.

At the very least, vote. Mail it in if you have to.

> If you're able to make someone smile,
> You've had a good day.
> If you're able to maintain that smile,
> You've had a good year.
> If you're able to make a difference,
> You've had a good life.
> We should all seek to enjoy the smiles in life.
> With the hope of one day making a difference.

> —Clayton Moore

I hope this book has encouraged and empowered you and helps as you decide how to serve and protect in your own way and in your own community. I'd love to connect with you and hope you'll follow or reach out to me through my website goodcopblackcop.com.

Finally, I'd appreciate it if you'll help me spread the message of this book by writing an honest review of this book on Amazon.

Thank you in advance for your time and effort and for everything you do to serve others and make the world we share a kinder, safer place for everyone in it.

APPENDIX

Select portions from FMCS Case No. 08-58518-8
Ohio Patrolmen's Benevolent Assn., Union vs. City of
Fostoria, Employer
Arbitrator Nels E. Nelson
Post-Hearing Brief of Union

Moore attended Fostoria High School, graduating in 1980, after spending his entire life in the city (Volume II of the Transcript of the Hearing in this matter ("Tr. Vol. II") p. 107). Moore excelled in football and was recently installed into the Fostoria High School Hall of Fame (Tr. Vol. II, p. 30). Moore attends the First Baptist Church of Fostoria where his family has worshiped for over forty years (Tr. Vol. II, pp. 70-71).

After graduating high school, Moore matriculated at the University of Toledo where he received a bachelor's degree in Communications in 1985. (Tr. Vol. II, p. 107).

Subsequent to receiving his college degree, Moore was hired by Fostoria High School as an assistant football coach.[1]

Moore was hired by the Fostoria Police Department in February 1986 as a police officer and served in that capacity until early in 2007 when he was promoted to sergeant (Tr. Vol. II, pp. 107-108).[2]

Moore had no record discipline in his personnel file at the time of his termination on August 5, 2008 (Tr. Vol. II, p. 108). Other than an approximately two-year stretch, Moore worked the midnight shift for virtually his entire career (Id.). After his promotion, Moore served as the midnight shift supervisor until he was assigned to the METRICH Drug Task Force late in calendar year 2007 (Id.).

Moore had an exemplary career, prior to the hiring of Police Chief John McGuire in or about February 2006 (Volume I of the transcript of the hearing in this matter ("Tr. Vol. I") p. 15).

Moore's problems began due to his role as spokesperson and Union Director for the Ohio Patrolmen's Benevolent Association ("OPBA") (Tr. Vol. II, pp. 178-183). In his role as Union Director, Moore was identified as a named plaintiff in a series of lawsuits filed by the OPBA to have McGuire removed as police chief, due to the illegal manner in which he was hired (Union Exhs. G, H & I).

Soon after McGuire's hiring by the city and the OPBA's filings to oust McGuire, Moore was subjected to a lengthy investigation and given a three-day suspension by McGuire. Moore grieved the discipline and was totally vindicated in arbitration (Union Exh. F; Tr. Vol I, pp. 314-315). The campaign by McGuire to seek retribution against Moore for his Union activity did not end there. First, in the fall of 2007, McGuire ignored his seniority shift bid and assigned Moore to METRICH, against his will, with the knowledge that the assignment would greatly interfere with Moore's ability to effectively function as a single parent[6] (Tr. Vol. II, p. 183).

Additionally, McGuire set Moore up to fail at METRICH by discussing uncorroborated, illusory prior "investigations" and/or allegations against Moore, with the drug task force supervisor Charles Boyer, prior to Moore's actual assignment to METRICH[7] (Tr. Vol. I, pp. 61-62).

In March 2008, Moore was summarily removed from the drug task force, without any due process, after an uncorroborated allegation by a female intern was communicated to Boyer and Joseph in late February 2008.[8]

Moore's reassignment to the day shift as a road patrol sergeant in March 2008, was simultaneous with McGuire's secret investigation of Moore concerning outdated and untimely issues. All of these purported complaints, with one exception, were solicited by McGuire.[9]

After McGuire's clandestine inquiries concerning Moore had progressed for approximately two months, McGuire hired a puppet named Arthur Marx, at $75 per hour, to implement his strategy to terminate Moore (Tr. Vol. I, pp. 99-100). Simultaneously, Moore was immediately placed on administrative leave on April 30, 2008 (Union Exh. B), and without being provided with warning or specific written allegations of wrongdoing, Moore was interviewed by Marx on that same day (Tr. Vol. I., pp. 110-111, 164-165). Moore answered Marx's question to the best of his ability given his lack of knowledge of the charges against him[10] (Er. Exh. 7).

Moore was ordered by the police chief to submit a written statement following his oral interview with Marx. Once again, Moore was still not aware of the specific charges against him when he submitted his written statement on May 2, 2008[11] (Jt. Exh. 6).

On or about May 21, 2008, Moore had an abbreviated second interview with Marx, at which time he attempted to clarify issues related to Moore's definition of "drugs" as compared to contraband or paraphernalia. Moreover, Moore attempted to clarify the time frame during which he had engaged in the well-accepted practice, prior to the hiring of McGuire, of disposing of minor amounts of contraband and/or paraphernalia by destroying them in the presence of another officer (Tr. Vol. I, pp. 16-17; Vol. II, pp. 166-168). Marx was purposefully obtuse concerning Moore's attempted clarification as it did not fit his and McGuire's theory of the case. In fact, Marx never put any of his findings and/or conclusions in writing, and he intentionally failed to summarize and submit to the city any interview containing information which tended to exonerate Moore (Tr. Vol. I, pp. 104-106, 108-110).

On or about July 30, 2008, a pre-disciplinary hearing was convened where, for the first time, Moore was presented with the specific charges against him (Tr. Vol. I, pp. 240-241; Jt. Exh. 10). Moore either provided information as to each allegation or relied on statements previously made in response to each of the allegations (Tr. Vol. I, pp. 240-244).

Subsequently, on or about August 6, 2008, Moore was terminated from his position at the Fostoria Police Department, without just cause and contrary to the principles of progressive discipline. Thereafter, a grievance was timely and properly processed to arbitration.

A hearing was commenced before this Arbitrator on October 27, 2008 and concluded on November 11, 2008. The parties agreed to submit post-hearing briefs on or before January 12, 2008.

The OPBA now timely submits this brief unequivocally illustrating that the grievance must be sustained.

IV. LAW AND ARGUMENT

A. General Legal Standard

"In this disciplinary proceeding, the burden of going forward and proving, by the preponderance of clear and convincing evidence, that it possessed 'just cause' for imposing" the discipline in this case rests upon the city. In the matter of Arbitration Between City of Cincinnati and FOP Queen City Lodge #69, 24 LAIS 2013, XII-51 (Arbitrator Langdon D. Bell, May 31, 1996).

Arbitrator Kapsch discussed the concept of just cause in light of its dictionary definition and other arbitration decisions and stated:

B. Moore's Due Process Rights Were Violated In This Case

At the hearing of this matter, the employer failed to produce all of the alleged complainants in this case. Namely, Employer Exhs. 5 and 6 reference a complaint by a person named Stephanie Dickson who made allegations against Moore that the City improperly characterized as "sexual harassment." Yet, Dickson was never produced as a witness in this case.

In addressing the impact of the above scenario on a grievant's due process rights in the pre-disciplinary and post-disciplinary action phases, Elkouri and Elkouri observed that it is permissible not to allow cross-examination in the pre-disciplinary phase. However, with respect to the post-disciplinary phase, the leading treatise on arbitration states as follows:

But if the grievant is never afforded the opportunity to cross-examine his or her accusers, even at a post-disciplinary arbitration hearing, due process has been violated. *Elkouri and Elkouri, How Arbitration Works*, 6th Ed. (BNA Books, 2003) at p. 1260.

If the arbitrator chooses not to find a violation of Moore's due process rights as stated above, he should at the very least, give little or no weight to the information related to Stephanie Dickson contained in Employer Exhibits 5 and 6 and in the testimony of Detectives Boyer and Joseph. This is especially true where, as here, Dickson refused to participate in the actual internal investigation and declined to be interviewed by the city's investigator. Moreover, all of the information referred to or provided by Dickson in Employer Exhs. 5 and 6 is unsubstantiated hearsay and must be disregarded by the arbitrator.

Moore's due process rights, as required by the CBA, were further violated by virtue of the fact that he was never provided with written notice of the specific allegations against him until the pre-disciplinary conference was convened on July 30, 2008. This violates Article 8, sections 5, 11, 12, and 13 of the CBA. Section 5 requires that "the employee shall be apprised of the alleged charge in writing, and a pre-disciplinary conference will be scheduled no sooner than forty-eight hours from the time of notice." As previously admitted by Chief McGuire, the specific allegations against Moore were never expressly set forth until during the pre-disciplinary conference itself (Tr. Vol. I, pp. 240-241). Article 8, Section 11 requires that "an employee will be informed as to the nature of any investigation of himself/herself prior to any questioning." A review of the transcript of Moore's investigatory in review contained in the record at Employer Exh. 7, illustrates that the only information given to Moore prior to his questioning was that "[t]he scope of this interview is to determine facts and statements concerning alleged violations of the policy, procedures, rules, regulations and directives of the Fostoria Police Department. You are being questioned for alleged violations of conduct unbecoming, sexual harassment, neglect of duty, harassment, allegations of misconduct" (Er. Ex. 7 at p. 3). This is significant in that the police chief tried to then claim that Moore's answers to the overbroad questions asked by Marx based on the above-stated vague allegations, were not complete or comprehensive enough. As there is no doubt that Moore was the last person interviewed by Marx, the city had more than enough information to properly inform Moore of the charges against him, yet it did not. Accordingly, their claim that Moore was somehow not completely truthful, smacks of bad faith on the city's part. Finally, Sections 12 and 13 of Article 8 require that the Employer will furnish copies of complaints to the Union and employee upon request, that the employer will produce any such complaints "in toto at any appropriate hearing, together with all evidence in its possession which applies to that complaint," and "the chief of police or his designee shall inform an employee against whom a complaint has been filed of the nature of the complaint and the outcome of any investigation within a reasonable time after completion of the investigation." The city did not comply with any of the foregoing requirements.

Furthermore, the city used the lack of specificity of the allegations to bring further charges against Moore by claiming that he was untruthful or that his answers in response to certain allegations changed over time. Of course they did. As Moore became aware of the specific incidents alleged, including the identity of persons involved and dates and times that matters were alleged to have occurred, he was able to provide further information concerning his actions. The city cannot use its own violations of Moore's contractual due process rights to fabricate additional allegations of dishonesty where none exist. These violations of the CBA's due process provisions, alone, require the grievance to be granted.

C. There Was No Just Cause For The Discipline In This Case And Principles Of Progressive Discipline Were Ignored

1. The City Failed To Prove That Moore Made A False Claim Or Misrepresentation In An Attempt To Obtain A City Benefit For Submitting An Overtime Slip On 5/21/08

On April 30, 2008, Moore was summarily placed on administrative leave with pay (Union Exh. B). At that time Moore was given a memo from Chief McGuire which stated as follows:

Per our conversation you are being placed on paid administrative leave pending completion of an internal investigation pertaining to the facts presented to you and your representative today. I will be securing your department issued side arm, keys, ID, and key card until completion of the internal investigation and you are reminded to not discuss the facts and circumstances of the pending case or investigation with other officers or potential witnesses. You are required to submit a written statement to me within (72) hours on the allegations involved. I will contact and update you on the status of the internal

investigation within seven days of receiving your state-
ment. Please advise if you have any questions or concerns
(Id.).

One can see from the above, there were no hours of work mentioned and no restrictions of any sort placed on Moore other than turning in his department issued side arm, keys, ID and key card until the completion of the investigation, and not discussing the facts and circumstances of the investigation with other officers or potential witnesses. It is undisputed that Moore had never previously been on administrative leave (Tr. Vol. II, p. 190). Moreover, Moore was unaware of any departmental rules or regulations governing administrative leave (Id.).

Thus, when Moore was ordered to appear at Arthur Marx's office in Toledo on May 21, 2008, Moore believed that it was in the nature of a call-in and that he was entitled to overtime under Article 10 of the CBA. Moore's belief was based, at least in part, on the fact that he had worked the midnight shift for more than twenty (20) years and any required work during daytime hours was nearly always overtime for him (Tr. Vol. II, p. 113).

Additionally, Moore's supervisor mistakenly approved the overtime, lending further credence to the fact that it might appear that Moore was entitled to overtime for his time spent pursuant to the order to report to Marx's office (Employer Exh. 10).

When Moore did not receive pay for the overtime, he called the undersigned requesting that a grievance be filed (Tr. Vol. II, p. 113). At that point, the undersigned explained to Moore that since he was on paid administrative leave and the obligation at Marx's office did not last more than eight hours, he was not entitled to overtime

(Tr. Vol. II, pp. 113-114). Moore accepted this explanation as reasonable, declined to file a grievance and did not attempt to pursue the matter any further. As Moore was never paid for the request, there was no harm done (Id.). Given the lack of information provided to Moore when he was placed on administrative leave, the fact he was never on such leave previously, the lack of departmental rules and regulations governing said leave, and the fact that a captain with 39 years of service initially approved the overtime, this was an obvious misunderstanding from which no harm resulted. As such, this charge should be dismissed by the arbitrator.

2. The City Failed To Meet Its Burden Of Proving That Moore Attempted The Misuse Of Confidential Information Without Authorization For His Attempt And Request For An Employee To Run A License Plate Through LEADS On 5/16/08 While On Administrative Leave.

As previously stated, all of the restrictions placed on Moore while on administrative leave are contained in Union Exh. B. Thus, Moore was never informed that he had no privileges as a Fostoria police officer. He was certainly not banned from the department, as the police chief acknowledged that he would converse with Moore at the police station during the period of time between April 30, 2008 when he was placed on administrative leave and the pre-disciplinary conference on July 30, 2008 (Tr. Vol. I, p. 236).

As such, when a citizen contacted Moore with a valid law enforcement-related request to discover the owner of a loose license plate found in his deceased son's vehicle,

Moore attempted to aid the citizen (Tr. Vol. II, pp. 92-93; 114-115).

The citizen, Mr. Dave Parker, who has worked for local businesses in Fostoria for many years, described his request, at the hearing ... (Tr. Vol. II, pp. 91-93).

In order to be responsive to a grieving local business person who was also a friend, Moore called the department, as he had done many times through the years and requested the dispatcher on duty to run the plate. (Tr. pp. 114-115). The dispatcher checked with Captain Brooks who denied Moore the privilege of running the plate because he was on administrative leave (Tr. Vol. I, p. 12).

According to Brook's [*sic*] when he told Moore that he would not permit the plate to be run, Moore was "nonplussed, he just said fine and hung up" (Id.). Brooks further acknowledged that it's not uncommon for an officer to call in to the department while off-duty and request that a license plate be run (Tr. Vol. I., p. 13). This was also verified by thirty-year dispatcher, Louanne Grine, who indicated that it wasn't at all unusual for off-duty officers to call in and request that a dispatcher run a registration or a license plate for just about any reason (Tr. Vol. II, pp. 83-84). Moreover, Captain Brooks acknowledged that Moore had a legitimate reason for wanting the plate run, but he didn't feel it was appropriate because Moore was on administrative leave (Tr. Vol. I, p. 14).

As a result, Moore, who was simply trying to assist a local business person with a legitimate request for assistance, is charged by the city with a purportedly serious rule violation.

The city produced no evidence that Moore was restricted from this type of activity while on administrative leave and Moore attempted the disputed action for benevolent purposes. The city has failed to sustain this charge, and thus, it should be dismissed.

3. The City Failed To Prove That Moore Engaged In Improper And Unauthorized Release Of Confidential Information For Telling A Third Party That Another Police Department Employee Had A Career Criminal History

The crux of this allegation is that Moore disclosed confidential information obtained from a LEADS printout dealing with Joanne Kitzler's prior criminal history, to a Fostoria municipal court employee named Karen Nesbitt.

The city miserably failed to meet its burden of proving that Moore ever accessed a confidential LEADS printout containing information about Kitzler's criminal history. Thus, Moore could not have released any such confidential information.

The only LEADS printout containing Kitzler's criminal history was processed by dispatcher Louanne Grine (Tr. Vol. I, pp. 256-257).

Moreover, the police chief admitted that he has no evidence that Moore ever reviewed a "CCH" involving Joanne Kitzler (Tr. Vol. I, p. 255).

Additionally, Grine lawfully and properly ran Kitzler's CCH as part of her duties as TAC Officer and in accordance with departmental policy (Tr. Vol. I, p. 257).

The results of the CCH run on Kitzler, by Grine, indicated that Kitzler had a criminal record for passing a bad check under her maiden name. Grine processed Kitzler's CCH to the police chief through Captain Deiter, but she never shared it or discussed it with Moore. (Tr. Vol. II, pp. 80-81). Grine did, however, hear rumors in the department of Kitzler's criminal record through overhearing other officers talking about it (Id.).

Moore verified that he never asked Grine to run a CCH on Kitzler, and he never saw a LEADS printout and/or a CCH that addressed that information. Any knowledge Moore had of Kitzler's criminal history was common knowledge gleaned through the rumor mill in the department (Tr. Vol. II, pp. 117-118).

Consequently, the police chief admits that he had no evidence that Moore ever had access to a LEADS printout or CCH of Kitzler, and thus, the charge that Moore disclosed confidential information cannot be sustained.

4. The City Failed To Prove That Moore Engaged In Threatening, Intimidating, Coercing Or Interfering With Other Employees For His Conversation Outside The Police Department In November 2007 With The Law Director

As an initial matter, there is no dispute that this conversation occurred when Moore was off-duty leaving the department after working out in November 2007. Yet, the law director, a licensed attorney and grown man, never disclosed any issue with this conversation until March 2008 (Tr. Vol. I, pp. 150, 172; Er. Exh. 9). Consequently, this charge should be dismissed as untimely, as a matter of law.

As a substantive matter, Hoover admitted that he initiated the conversation with Moore in November 2007, while Moore was in plain clothes and off-duty with no visible weapon on his person (Tr. Vol. I, p. 150). Hoover also acknowledged that his previous dealings with Moore had always been "very cordial, very easy going," as Moore is a very likeable person who Hoover has always enjoyed talking to (Tr. Vol. I, p. 141).

Additionally, Hoover characterized Moore as a guy who always has a smile on his face and who "will go out of his way to be nice to you" (Id.). Further, Hoover admitted that the particular conversation, at issue, consisted initially of small talk and that the conversation was "jovial" and "cordial" (Tr. Vol. I, pp. 139-140).

Finally, Hoover testified that the end of the conversation, just before they departed, consisted of talking football (Id.)

The alleged wrongful conduct by Moore was in response to a question asked by Hoover which Hoover described as an inquiry into "if there are any issues with the prosecutor's office, basically how can we help you sort of conversation" (Tr. Vol. I, p. 139), (Tr. Vol. II, pp. 121-122).

Thus, the city wants to discipline Moore for answering another city elected official's questions nine months after the conversation occurred and under the circumstances that the law director never complained about the tone or the substance of the conversation until many months later. Under the totality of the circumstances, the city has not even remotely proven that Moore threatened, intimidated, coerced or interfered with other employees. That is especially true in that Hoover asked the question that led to the answer that was purportedly objectionable. Employees should not be disciplined for honestly answering questions put to them by city officials, especially when the employee is off-duty and is engaged by the other party to the conversation. This charge cannot be sustained. Finally, Hoover admitted that he had no evidence that Moore influenced anyone on his shift or that Moore changed his own personal work habits to the detriment of the city after their conversation in November 2007 (Tr. Vol. I, p. 174).

5. Moore Did Not Engage In Conduct Unbecoming For Personal Involvement In Another Officer's Case And He Did Not Interfere With His Brother's Case By Telephoning A Prosecutor And Asking For A Recognizance Bond

As an initial matter, there is no evidence, whatsoever, that Moore somehow became personally involved in the investigation of another officer's case.

The record reflects that Moore's brother, Damon, was involved in a physical altercation in a local bar in the city of Fostoria.

This matter was investigated by Fostoria Police Officer Cory Echelberry.

First, the city did not produce Officer Echelberry to testify at the hearing of this matter. Second, Marx testified that he interviewed Echelberry but decided not to memorialize and provide a written summary of Echelberry's interview to the city and/or the union. Finally, Marx testified that Echelberry did not disclose information sufficient to support a conclusion that Moore interfered in the investigation of his brother, Damon (Tr. Vol. I, p.105). Thus, consistent with its mode of operation in this case, the city attempted to hide any potential exculpatory evidence concerning Moore's alleged conduct.

In any event, Moore tried to stay as far away from the investigation of his brother as possible so as not to allow even the appearance of impropriety (Tr. Vol. II, p. 124). He did not review any reports or in any way exert supervisory authority with respect to his brother's case.

He left the station when his brother was interviewed, he encouraged his brother to participate in the investigation, he did not give any input as to what charge, if any, should be filed and he eventually informed his brother, who was living in Columbus, that there was a warrant for his arrest and that he needed to return to Fostoria to address it (Tr. Vol. II, pp. 124-127). Finally, Moore did not have any input into the grand jury process and did not even attend his brother's arraignment, disposition or sentencing hearing (Tr. Vol. II, pp. 130-132). Thus, as previously described, Moore attempted to totally separate himself from the investigation, charging, processing and disposition of his brother's case. This was verified by Law Director Hoover who testified that other than one brief phone call, he had no evidence, nor reasonable inference that Moore interfered in the prosecution of his brother's case (Tr. Vol. I, p. 167).

The reference in this allegation to the phone call to prosecutors refers to an inquiry by Moore as to what the possible bond conditions were going to be for his brother's case.

The summary of Assistant Prosecutor Carol Reffner's interview with Marx indicates that she was originally assigned to the prosecution of Moore's brother (Union Exh. C). She typed up the charges against Damon Moore (Union Exh. C, paragraph 2). She described her phone conversation with Moore in Union Exh. C, as follows:

1. Sergeant Clayton Moore called Mrs. Raffner [*sic*] sometime after the warrant was issued. He was aware of the charge, and he asked about his brother turning himself in. He stated that he knew his brother really screwed up and he told

him that. He also stated that his brother was going to turn himself in.

2. Mrs. Reffner reminded the sergeant of the days for arraignment in court and suggested that it would look really good if he came in on his own because the judge usually releases people on their own recognizance when they turn themselves in and they are not a risk.

3. Mrs. Reffner told Mrs. Dibble that she did not promise anything to Clayton, however the usual thing would happen when someone turns themselves in.

4. Mrs. Reffner had previously told Sergeant Moore that she would recommend the OR bond if his brother turned himself in and she did not find any do not appears or other outstanding issues.

5. Mrs. Reffner did not have any other conversations with Sergeant Moore about his brother. She suspected that Sergeant Moore may have felt a little betrayed when his brother was not released.

6. Mrs. Reffner regrets the situation regarding the own recognizance bond because she did give Sergeant Moore the impression that if she were in charge she would have recommended the bond, however, the final decision would have to be made by the judge.

Reffner's recollection of the phone conversation does not suggest that Moore was somehow out of line when he contacted her. Instead, she expressed regret over the situation because she gave Moore the impression that she would recommend the OR Bond. This is not consistent with a situation where someone is attempting to influence or interfere with a decision in an untoward manner.

Instead, this is consistent with Moore's explanation for the phone call which was that he called Carol Reffner, a person that he has known for nearly 30 years, and asked if there was a chance that his brother would be released on his own recognizance, or not, so that his family could raise the money if there was going to be a cash bond. Moore did not attempt to influence the decision as to what the bond would be, but only wanted to inform his family members of how much cash they might need (Tr. Vol. II, pp. 127-128).

Moore did make a second call to the prosecutor's office to notify Reffner of when his brother would appear to turn himself in. At that time, he spoke to Hoover, who indicated that he was not intimidated by anything Moore said during that brief discussion and that nothing Moore said influenced his decision with respect to the appropriate bond recommendation (Tr. Vol. I, pp. 163-164). Further, Hover [*sic*] never brought this conversation to the police chief's attention until more than two months after the conversation occurred. Finally, both Reffner's and Hoover's testimony refutes the city's contention that Moore left "a note requesting an OR bond" for his brother, as both of the prosecutors verified that Reffner is the one who left the note for Hoover (Tr. Vol. I, p. 159; Union Exh. C).

To this day, the police chief is adamant that Moore wrote the note, despite all evidence to the contrary (Tr. Vol. I, p. 202).

The foregoing unequivocally demonstrates that the city did not meet its burden of proving the charges addressed in this section.

6. Moore Did Not Threaten, Intimidate, Coerce And/Or Interfere With Other Employees For His Actions During A Conversation With Law Director Hoover On 1/23/08 At The Sececa [*sic*] County Courthouse

This allegation was refuted by the testimony of every witness with knowledge of the incident, including Hoover himself.

As an initial matter, this complaint was solicited by the police chief in March 2008, two months after the conversation occurred. This is evidenced by the fact that the law director wrote a letter containing his rendition of the conversation which is dated March 14, 2008 (Er. Exh. 9). The letter itself makes it clear that it is being written upon request from the chief, and Hoover testified that "Absolutely, no, I didn't want to write this" (Tr. Vol. I, pp. 150, 175).

Hoover begins his letter with a disclaimer—"the following recollections are based solely on my memory, as I did not make notes on the matter." He then continues by totally twisting the facts. Hoover contends that "Sgt. Moore accused me in front of members of the public, as well as members of the Drug Task force (e.g. Don Joseph and Chuck Boyer) and Ken Egbert's office (e.g., Ken Clason), of lying to him" (Er. Exh. 9).

The city produced no members of the public or employees of the prosecutor's office who overheard the conversation. Chuck Boyer, one of the drug task force members who allegedly overheard the conversation, testified that, in fact, he never overheard any discussion between Hoover and Moore at the Seneca county courthouse (Tr. Vol. I, pp. 86-87). Detective Don Joseph testified that Hoover approached him and Moore and that they were being quiet, speaking in low tones (Tr. vol. II, p. 43). He further indicated that it was only Hoover, Moore and Joseph present, no member of the public was present and that Moore was not aggressive in his demeanor toward Hoover (Id.). In fact, Hoover, himself, wrote that Moore's attitude was not confrontational (Er. Exh. 9).

Moreover, once again, Hoover admitted that he initiated the conversation with Moore at the courthouse and that he requested that Moore discuss the issues further with him by inviting Moore into a conference room where Hoover then closed the door (Tr. Vol. I, pp. 143, 168).

Hoover and Moore then further discussed Moore's feeling that Hoover lied to him about his brother's bond recommendation, at which point the discussion ended. Despite the fact that Hoover now apparently believes that Moore committed some egregious violation of some illusory employment rule, Hoover wrote on March 14, 2008, that "I understood his concern" (Er. Exh. 9)

Once again, the city wants to discipline Moore for an issue, unrelated to his job, that would never have arisen if a city official had not initiated a conversation with him. Further, Hoover's version of the event was obviously exaggerated and not corroborated by the one objective third party witness. The fact that Hoover and McGuire have conspired to adversely impact Moore's employment with the city is supported by the amount of time that passed between the occurrence of the incidents and the reporting of the incidents, but it is also made crystal clear by Hoover's testimony at the hearing to the effect that the conversations that he had with Moore have caused him to make sure that his doors are properly locked and the gates to his backyard are locked at night (Tr. Vol. II, p. 147). This over-dramatization of these events, in light of Hoover's own pervious [sic] description of these events, in conjunction with Joseph's and Moore's recollection, leads one to the obvious conclusion that much of the city's evidence, with respect to this and other allegations, was contrived. The city has failed to substantiate this allegation.

7. The City Has Failed To Prove That Moore Ever Took "Narcotics" Off Of Suspects Without 1) Logging Them Into Evidence, 2) Making An Arrest or Citation Or Making A Report

This charge is a classic example of the police chief attempting to pile on a mountain of charges, after the fact, in an all-out effort to justify the unsupportable recommendation of termination in this case.

Marx's original statement of the charges to Moore on April 30, 2008, did not reference any alleged allegations concerning "narcotics," at all (Er. Exh. 7 at p. 3).

At the hearing, however, Marx indicated that two of the original allegations against Moore were drug related. First, Marx explained that one allegation was "about him purchasing drugs on the street, having a witness who knew him personally, and that Keith Miller or Keith whatever his name is, I have to find the file, he was known as K-Boo, that the witness observed him pay $50" (Tr. Vol. I, pp. 101-102). Another allegation concerned a Mr. Smith and a concern that Moore somehow took drugs from a Mr. Smith but did not arrest him. Both of these incidents purportedly occurred eight years earlier in calendar year 2000 (Er. Exh. 7 at pp. 70-71).

When asked whether K-Boo was interviewed in his investigation, Marx explained that "[w]e're not able to find him. He's in and out of jail and in and out of prison, and so it—it was a dead-end. We weren't able to find him." (Tr. Vol. I, p. 106). Similarly, Mr. Smith was unable to be located (Id.). Marx further indicated that there was no corroborating evidence concerning the allegations related to Smith, so he essentially dropped that area of inquiry (Tr. Vol. I, p. 92).

At the end of the day, the city admitted that it had no proof that either of the allegations concerning K-Boo or Mr. Smith could be proven and those charges were dropped.

Although the city could not prove its eight-year old allegations concerning K-Boo and Mr. Smith, it did not simply drop the line of inquiry totally. Instead, the police chief manufactured other charges, after the investigation was concluded, by twisting testimony given by Moore during the internal investigation on May 21, 2008, and again at the pre-disciplinary conference on July 30, 2008.

On this topic, a discussion was had with Mr. Marx on May 21, 2008, where it was explained to Mr. Marx that Moore had served under five (5) different police chiefs, and the accepted practice during that time permitted the officers to take contraband from suspects, destroy the contraband by flushing it or putting it down the sewer and that this usually involved small amounts of marijuana or seeds. Moore then clarified that he had not participated in this type of action since McGuire became chief. (Union Exh. D). This is consistent with Moore's representation at the pre-disciplinary conference where he clarified that the destruction of drugs referred to marijuana seeds or a half of a joint—something small like that and that it had been a practice in the department previously (Jt. Exh. 10).

This was confirmed by Captain Pat Brooks ... (Tr. Vol. I, pp. 16-17).

Thus, for his honesty in admitting that, pursuant to longstanding departmental practice prior to the hiring of McGuire, he disposed of small amounts of contraband on occasion, Moore is charged with taking "narcotics" off of suspects without logging them into evidence, etc.

Moreover, the implication by the city throughout this process is that Moore had confiscated "drugs" for his own personal use.

There is no evidence in the record of this case that Moore ever took "narcotics" from a suspect and destroyed them or in any way converted them to his own use. The record is clear that Moore does not use drugs and/or alcohol and that in fact, Moore is a staunch advocate against drug and alcohol abuse.

This allegation was untimely and unsupported in the record and cannot be sustained.

8. Moore Did Not Publish False, Vicious Or Malicious Statements About Employees Or City Operations And Did Not Create A Hostile Working Environment Including Sexual Harassment For Allegedly Slanderous, Malicious, Inaccurate Comments Made About A Specific Female Police Department Employee

One immediate clue as to the facts that the evidence against Moore is weak and that the allegations are over-blown is the way that the allegations are worded. The frequent use of the terms "false," "malicious," "vicious," "slanderous" and the consistent misrepresentation of certain purported conduct as "sexual harassment" totally belies the alleged seriousness of these charges.

All of the record evidence surrounding these five loaded charges is contained in two brief private conversations between long-time friends. Specifically, the allegations arose from two conversations between Moore and Fostoria municipal court employee, Karen Nesbitt, in April 2008 (Er. Exh. 2).

The timing of these conversations is significant because by then Moore had been summarily transferred back from the METRICH Drug Task Force, without due process, and he was aware that he was under internal investigation. Despite these facts, there is no evidence that Moore denigrated the police chief or the police department during these conversations. The only written record evidence on these topics is that Moore generally indicated that things in the department were, at that time, difficult for him and that he may have said something about the chief, but it was unintelligible (Er. Exh. 2).

In her testimony, Nesbitt indicated that she has known Moore for fifteen years and they have had a very good relationship (Tr. Vol. I, p. 23). Through the years, Nesbitt and Moore spoke to each other frequently, both on and off duty (Tr. Vol. I, p. 28). These discussions occasionally were about their jobs (Id.).

The two discussions at issue occurred briefly as Nesbitt was returning from lunch with her husband. Her husband's vehicle was positioned in the city lot and Moore pulled in behind them. Both discussions were similar in content (Tr. Vol. I., p. 26). Nesbitt approached Moore's car when he entered the lot and pulled behind her husband because she and Moore are friends (Tr. Vol. I, p. 24). Moore remained in his vehicle as they spoke. Moore made a general comment about things being difficult in the police department; he did not elaborate on anything (Tr. Vol. I., pp. 24-25). If Moore said something about the police chief, Nesbitt did not comprehend it because he was mumbling and it was said under his breath. (Tr. Vol. I, pp. 24-25, 34). Thus, the city has not proven that Moore made false, vicious or malicious statements about "city operations" and it has not proven by any stretch of the imagination that Moore stated "how bad it was working at the police department, under the chief and bimbo he had working for him, the bullshit going on at the department under the chief and that the chief should not be the chief." This last quotation is taken directly from Allegations #3, 4, 5, 7 in Jt. Exh. 4, and it is illustrative of the consistent fabrication of charges against Moore. The police chief included that quotation directly in the charges as having been proven by the city, yet, Nesbitt, the only witness to these allegations, never claimed that Moore made any of those alleged quoted statements.

Since Nesbitt and Moore were the only parties to the conversation and neither one of them gave testimony supporting the quoted charge, then it had to have been made up. This type of conduct by the city cannot be sanctioned by this arbitrator.

As to the remainder of the specific charges, Moore is accused of referring to a police department employee as a "bimbo" and stating that a department employee had "a conviction for forgery or a felony." Moreover, those alleged statements by Moore are purported to have created "a hostile work environment including sexual harassment" for allegedly uttering the foregoing statements.

The conversations between Moore and Nesbitt were meant by Moore to be private conversations between friends. He was in his car, Nesbitt was leaning in to the car window (Tr. Vol. II, p. 141). Moore was frustrated about the treatment of him related to his transfer back from METRICH and the treatment of him generally by the chief. Moore vented that the chief's administrative assistant and confidante, Joanne Kitzler, was an airhead or was flighty (Id.). Moore regurgitated, to Nesbitt only, that the department rumor mill indicated that Kitzler had a past conviction possibly for felony forgery (Jt. Exh. 6). Moore never saw a LEADS report concerning Kitzler, "it was just office chatter" (Id.).

Moore never directly approached Kitzler about her criminal history, he never degraded her in any manner to her face, and he never said anything about Kitzler publicly or to anyone other than Nesbitt (Tr. Vol. I, pp. 139-141; Jt. Exh. 6). This was verified by both Nesbitt (Tr. Vol. I, p. 32) and Kitzler, herself, who indicated that no one else other than Nesbitt ever approached her about what Moore allegedly said (Tr. vol. I, p. 41). Finally, Nesbitt intended to relay Moore's comments to Kitzler in private, and Kitzler admitted that she desired that Holly Cassady also hear what Nesbitt told her (Tr. Vol. I, pp. 33, 42-43).

While Moore may have not exercised perfect judgment in confiding his frustration in a long-term friend, the facts and circumstances indicate that he was not acting in a malicious, vicious or slanderous manner.

Finally, the allegation that Moore's purported characterization of Kitzler as a "bimbo," which Moore steadfastly denies, could somehow arise to the level of a hostile work environment and/or sexual harassment is ridiculous. The record is clear that, despite the police chief's convenient memory lapse to the contrary, Kitzler, herself, has been the subject of a complainant claiming sexual harassment against her (Union Exh. J). Additionally, Captain Brooks testified that Kitzler often flirts with the younger male employees; that she has scantly [*sic*] clad male models displayed on her desk top computer; she has given gifts to male employees on special occasions, including the reference to the male(s) as "hot stuff," and that she has engaged in sexual banter with other employees, possibly including Moore (Tr. Vol. II, pp. 73-76). As such, the private characterization of Kitzler as a "bimbo," if it occurred, does not in any way amount to sexual harassment and/or the creation of a hostile work environment.

The city has failed to meet its burden of proving that allegations #3, 4, 5, 7, and 12 amount to conduct adequate to support the termination of Moore.

9. The City Has Not Proven That Moore Created A Hostile Work Environment And Sexual Harassment For Actions And Conduct Unbecoming On 2/28/08 With A Specific Female Intern While Assigned To The METRICH Drug Task Force

As an initial matter and as previously asserted, the pseudo-complainant concerning this charge has never been interviewed as part of the actual investigation of Moore and she did not appear to testify at the hearing of this matter. As a result, Moore's absolute right to confront and cross-examine his accuser was violated and this charge should be immediately dismissed.

If not, no weight, whatsoever, should be given to any of the hearsay evidence (Er. Exhs. 5 and 6) on this topic which the arbitrator permitted to be introduced into the record evidence in this matter.

The only persons who actually interacted with Stephanie Dickson more than one month after the alleged incident occurred–Detectives Boyer and Joseph, indicated that they were not conducting an investigation of the allegations (Tr. Vol. I, pp. 79-80; Tr. Vol. II, p. 55). Moreover, Detective Joseph testified that with respect to the allegations against Moore, he had no reasons to disbelieve Moore's version of the events (Tr. Vol. II, p. 66).

As Dickson did not testify, this arbitrator has no possible way to evaluate her credibility or motives. As such, Moore's testimony on this topic is undisputed in the record of this case …

Moore's recollection matched that of Detective Joseph who remembered that during the drug buy which preceded the car ride that prompted Dickson's allegations a drug suspect left the surveilled residence in a manner that initially suggested that their cover was blown (Tr. Vol. II, p. 47). This prompted discussion among Moore, Joseph, and Dickson concerning counter-surveillance techniques (Tr. Vol. II, pp. 48-49). Consequently, Moore's explanation of what occurred later during his conversation with Dickson on the ride back to Tiffin is eminently reasonable.

Finally, Dickson, herself, did not even wish to pursue a charge of sexual harassment against Moore. Joseph testified that "she kept saying to me that she didn't want Clayton to get in any trouble." She also provided information that this was a one-time incident where Moore never touched her or threatened her in any way and for which she had no tangible evidence or records of the alleged incident (Er. Exh. 6). Based on those facts, the METRICH Board decided not to further investigate the allegations (Tr. Vol. II, p. 55).

Even though this was one of the flagship allegations against Moore, the city did nothing to investigate the charge. Instead, it delegated the investigation to two task force detectives who played no role in the internal investigation of Moore and who both clearly indicated that the allegations against Moore were unsubstantiated.

Finally, this alleged conduct of Moore does not meet the city of Fostoria's definition of sexual harassment which states:

> *Sexual harassment may include unwelcome sexual advances, requests for sexual favors, or other verbal or physical contact of a sexual nature when such conduct creates an offensive, hostile and intimidating working environment and prevents an individual from effectively performing the duties of their position. It also encompasses such conduct when it is made a term or condition of employment or compensation, either implicitly or explicitly and when an employment decision is based on an individual's acceptance or rejection of such conduct (Er. Exh. 12).*

Dickson, who was not an employee of the city or METRICH, never even alleged that Moore's conduct amounted to "unwelcome sexual advances, requests for sexual favors, or other verbal or physical contact of a sexual nature." Moreover, she definitely never alleged that Moore's conduct created an "offensive, hostile or intimidating work environment" or that it prevented her from effectively performing her duties." Instead, she alleged that she felt "uncomfortable" (Tr. Vol. II, p. 57), but not to the extent that she desired to file a formal charge supported by a signed "detailed description of all events," as required by the city's own sexual harassment investigation criteria (Er. Exh. 6). Finally, Dickson refused to talk to Marx and was not produced as a witness at the arbitration hearing by the city.

The city has miserably failed to meet its burden of proving this charge, and thus, it cannot be sustained.

> 10. There Is No Record Evidence That Moore Disregarded Rules, Regulations, Policies Or Procedures On 12/31/07 In Making A Traffic Stop Without Calling Same Into Dispatch Or Over Radio Or For Allegedly Operating A Vehicle In An Unsafe Manner

This is another of the allegations that were created by the police chief and for which Moore's contractual due process rights were violated. Initially, this charge was never conveyed to Marx by the police chief as any area of concern. Moreover, Moore was never informed of this allegation specifically, until the pre-disciplinary conference on July 30, 2008, despite the fact that the police chief had knowledge of it in December 2007. Further, even though it happened on December 3, 2007, and McGuire sanctioned a surreptitious investigation of Moore at that time by a junior subordinate, McGuire did not have the "investigator" memorialize his findings until months later on March 9, 2008 (Er. Exh. 8).

Specifically, McGuire had a junior patrol officer–Matt Armstrong, who had a tenuous relationship with Moore, secretly following Moore and documenting his activities on the early morning of December 3, 2007. Furthermore, resources of the State of Ohio, through the actions of a state trooper, were also wrongly utilized in this effort to implicate Moore (Id.).

Unfortunately, if McGuire had simply shared Armstrong's complaint with Moore, as he is required to do by the CBA, all of this would have been avoided!

The actual record evidence indicates that, Gayle Martin, a twenty-year family friend of Moore's and a colleague and fellow worshiper, who worked on a committee together with Moore at their church, was on her way to work at approximately 2:00 a.m. on the morning of December 3, 2007, when she spotted Moore at a gas station convenience store across from her apartment (Tr. Vol. II, pp. 5-7). Martin desired to talk to Moore to inform him that she would miss a church committee meeting later that day, but she needed to stop at the bank and didn't want to be late for work. Martin had, however, somehow gotten Moore's attention, as he proceeded to pull behind her on Route 199, where she pulled her car over, due to the fact that his bright headlights were in her eyes through a reflection in her mirror (Tr. pp. 7-8). Moore activated his overhead lights, for safety reasons, and exited his vehicle to speak with Martin. He approached her vehicle on foot and had a brief conversation, including the fact that she would not be present at the church finance committee meeting later that day and that she was on her way to the bank (Id.). Moore followed her to the bank to assure her safety, since it was 2:00 a.m. and then he left and she continued onto work (Tr. Vol. II, p. 9).

As Moore did not initiate a traffic stop and he was simply having a brief discussion with a long-term friend about church business, Moore did not violate any policies, rules and/or procedures during the early morning of December 3, 2007.

This charge was initiated without adequate investigation and for malicious purposes. It was untimely and is clearly unproven. Moreover, the chief's conduct in soliciting this improper investigation by a subordinate officer on Moore's shift and then failing to memorialize the entire incident until three months later is outrageous. This charge cannot be sustained.

11. Moore Did Not Willfully Fail To Make Required Reports After Answering Being Assigned And Handling An Alleged Fight At And Lockdown Of Fostoria School

This is another in the line of charges fabricated by the police chief. The incident at Fostoria High School that prompted this charge occurred in the morning of April 29, 2008. Moore was assigned by his captain to remain at the high school for the remainder of that day and was immediately placed on administrative leave on April 30, 2008 (Union Exh. B). Not only was Moore placed on administrative leave on April 30, 2008, but he was also extensively interviewed by Marx on that same date (Er. Exh. 7). Thus, even if Moore was required to do a report as to the April 29, 2008 incident, which he expressly was not, he was relieved of duty immediately upon returning from his day-long assignment at the high school on the previous day and was therefore not permitted to complete the report. One must remember that another of the charges against Moore here is that he tried to run a license plate, while on administrative leave. That conduct was wrongful according to Captain Brooks, due to the fact that he was on administrative leave which "precluded him from accessing our equipment and resources" (Tr. Vol. I, p. 14).

The facts of the incident at Fostoria High School were also not as the police chief presented them. Fostoria High School Principal Jude Meyers, explained that a female student confronted two male students and a verbal altercation occurred. However, there wasn't any fight and no physical altercation of any sort ensued (Tr. Vol. II, p. 17-18). While Meyers explained that the police were called, the matter had deescalated by the time the police arrived (Tr. Vol. II, pp. 19-20). Moreover, no criminal charges were sought by the school over the incident, and Meyers did not require any assistance from the police after their arrival (Tr. Vol. II, pp. 21-23).

The police response on that date consisted of two senior captains—Deiter and Brenner, plus Moore (Er. Exh. 14).

The original narrative, which closed the case at that time, indicates that the "disturbance was between boyfriend and girlfriend. No injuries involved. FHS was put in lockdown by school authorities. Sergeant Moore was stationed at the school for the remainder of the day" (Union Exh. E, p. 3; Er. Exh. 14). The foregoing entry by a dispatcher should have been sufficient to close the case at that point in time. As Louanne Grine, a thirty-year dispatcher, explained, "a lot of times if the officers brought in a call and they'd go ahead and tell me to go ahead and close out the call, nothing was going on, put the disposition..." They'd go ahead and they'd tell me what the disposition was and I'd close them out" (Tr. Vol. II, pp. 82-83). Captain Brooks further explained that, "if you're on duty, dispatcher receives a call. You get dispatched on it, you handle your call if its [sic] of no—there's not going to be a report, I mean a case file done, you're able to resolve the situation, you call in the disposition to the dispatcher, the dispatcher types in your disposition and closes the call" (Tr. Vol. I, p. 18). Brooks continued by indicating that while that practice had changed it did not change until May or June, 2008 (Tr. Vol. I, p. 19).

Thus, on April 29, 2008, Moore properly closed out the case by indicating the disposition to the dispatcher who typed in the disposition previously set forth, which is contained in Union Exh. E and Employer Exh. 14.

Because this was concerning Moore, however, the police chief, in an effort to create further charges to support his termination, instructed Captain Deiter to require further investigation. Thus, on May 4, 2008, Deiter wrote a memo to DARE Officer Matt Noftz ... (Union Exh. E) (Emphasis supplied).

Although the police chief designated this "follow-up investigation" of the utmost importance, no further substantive information was discovered until May 15, 2008, when Police Officer Shilo Frankart filed a one-sentence "*narrative*" which closed out the case as follows: "Mr. Meyers advised that the incident will be handled internally. No further assistance will be needed by the police department" (Employer Exh. 14).

Moore was assigned to remain at the school by Captain Brenner for the rest of his shift on April 29, 2008. Moore was immediately placed on administrative leave and sent for investigative interview conducted by Marx on the very next day—April 30, 2008. Moore properly closed out the case at the high school by giving the disposition to the dispatcher who entered a narrative pursuant to the then-current practice. Moore believed that he had then closed the file (Tr. Vol. II, p. 63). No one instructed Moore to perform any further follow-up on the case prior to being placed on administrative leave (Tr. Vol. II, p. 176). When the DARE officer, Matt Noftz was instructed to perform further follow-up, he did not do it. When further follow-up was allegedly done more than two weeks later by Officer Shilo Frankart, it was amazingly discovered that the school desired to handle the incident internally and no further assistance by the police department was needed.

This charge was created by the police chief, after-the-fact, to attempt to support the unreasonable decision to terminate Moore in this case.

The actual facts in evidence do not support wrongdoing by Moore in not filing a further report with respect to the incident at the Fostoria High School on April 29, 2008. This charge cannot be sustained.

12. The City Failed To Meet Its Burden Of Proving That Moore Was Somehow Not Honest Or That He Gave False Testimony During The Investigation Of A Complaint

As is his wont, the police chief, after setting forth numerous specific charges of alleged wrongdoing against Moore in Jt. Exh. 4, and concluding that "it is for these substantiated Group 3 and Group 2 violations that I must recommend his immediate termination," then tosses in for good measure the vague, overbroad and unsupported statement that, "[t]here is also substantial evidence and numerous additional counts of {Giving false testimony during the investigation of a complaint}..."

Of course, when requested to specifically identify this substantial evidence and numerous additional counts of "giving false testimony," at the hearing of this matter, the police chief stuttered, stammered and tried to avoid answering the question at all costs, before finally indicating that "I can't tell you for sure. I'd be guessing, and I don't want to do that. At some point during the investigation that's when these number of inconsistencies and lies came forward" (Tr. Vol. I, pp. 244-245).

At one point, McGuire did claim that the submission of the overtime slip, after being placed on administrative leave, and some vague assertion concerning the unproven allegation related to the purported taking of "narcotics," without a report, constituted the "false testimony" given by Moore during the investigation (Tr. Vol. I, pp. 242-243). These contentions have been sufficiently refuted elsewhere in this brief.

McGuire finally admitted that the universe of record evidence from which these alleged false statements were purportedly given, consisted of Moore's initial interview by Marx memorialized in Er. Exh. 7; the written statement provided by Moore in response to the chief's order which is in the record in Joint Exh. 6; the second interview with Marx, the substantive portion of which is contained in Union Exh. D; and the pre-disciplinary conference verbatim transcript which is in the record at Jt. Exh. 10 (Tr. Vol. I, p. 245).

If one reviews these exhibits, which are the complete universe of record evidence on this topic, with a jaundiced eye, one discovers that there is absolutely no evidence of false testimony or attempted deception by Moore.

Rather, one discovers a twenty-three-year veteran police officer with a clean disciplinary history and an excellent reputation in the community who is falsely accused of numerous vaguely-stated improper acts over an unspecified time period spanning his entire career. Certainly, when faced with responding to these types of allegations, a person's answers may evolve or require clarification once the accuser finally specifies dates, times and the identity of other persons allegedly involved. In fact, Moore tried to the best of his ability to provide accurate and comprehensive information on each topic by supplementing and/or clarifying the record as the charges were stated to him with further specificity (Tr. Vol. II, pp. 166-170). The vast majority of allegations against Moore were never stated with any specificity until after the investigation was over and the pre-disciplinary conference was convened.

The city had the burden of proving that Moore's testimony was somehow dishonest or false and it expressly did not. In fact, McGuire clearly testified that at the initiation of the investigation of Moore, there were only two charges being investigated and the rest "evolved" from that point forward (Tr. Vol. I, p. 247). To the extent that this charge was even relied on in terminating Moore, which his [sic] doubtful upon a careful reading of Jt. Exh. 4, it cannot be sustained.

IV. CONCLUSION

For the foregoing reasons, the grievance should be granted in full. The grievant should be made whole, the disciplinary action should be rescinded and all evidence of the discipline should be removed from any employment-related file.[1]

NOTES

Prologue

[1] Review Times. "Officer's personnel file loaded with allegations." Chandra Niklewski. Fostoria, Ohio. Wednesday edition. August 20, 2008. Print.

Chapter 1

[1] Review Times. "Fostoria's Top Sports Figures." Steve Banks. Fostoria.org.
http://fostoria.org/index.php/2012-05-14-15-26-09/fostoria-s-top-sports-figures

Chapter 2

[1] Equal Employment Opportunity Commission (EEOC). Executive Order 10925. Establishing the President's Committee on Equal Employment Opportunity. March 6, 1961. John F. Kennedy.
https://www.eeoc.gov/eeoc/history/35th/thelaw/eo-10925.html

Chapter 5

[1] UMKC School of Law. Professor Douglas O. Linder. Famous Trials: Closing Arguments of Johnnie Cochran (excerpts).
https://famous-trials.com/simpson/1868-cochranclosing

2   Bible Hub. New American Standard Version of the Holy
    Bible (NASB).
    https://biblehub.com/proverbs/18-17.htm

Chapter 6

1   Diangelo, Robin. *White Fragility: Why It's So Hard for
    White People to Talk about Racism.* Beacon Press. Boston,
    Massachusetts. 2018. Print. p. 100.
2   Affidavit of Probable Cause to Charge George
    Zimmerman with Second Degree Murder. SCRIBD.
    https://www.scribd.com/doc/89112477/Affidavit-of-
    Probable-Cause-to-charge-George-Zimmerma
    n-with-second-degree-murder?campaign=Ski
    mbitLtd&ad_group=35871X943606Xc6ba460b-
    80197d94ea572da44ea67ead&keyword=660149026&-
    source=hp_affiliate&medium=affiliate

Chapter 8

1 *Toledo News.* WTOL11. "Fostoria Police Chief Indicted."
    October 19, 2006, updated June 30, 2018. Accessed
    November 11, 2020.
    https://www.wtol.com/article/news/fostoria-police-
    chief-indicted/512-b042632d-7c0c-41d3-864d-
    9a051bdb83b8
2   Supreme Court of Ohio Case No. 2008-0720. State Ex.
    Rel. James Deiter et al. vs. Police Chief John McGuire
    et al. Filed July 28, 2008. (Court of Appeals Case No.
    13-07-23.)
3   FMCS Case No. 08-58518-8 In the Federal Mediation
    and Conciliation Services. Ohio Patrolmen's Benevolent
    Assn., Union vs. City of Fostoria, Employer. Arbitrator
    Nels E. Nelson. 19 January 2019. (Appendix)

Chapter 10

[1] Review Times. "Officer's personnel file loaded with allegations." Chandra Niklewski. Fostoria, Ohio. Wednesday edition. August 20, 2008. Print.

[2] FMCS Case No. 08-58518-8 In the Federal Mediation and Conciliation Services. Ohio Patrolmen's Benevolent Assn., Union vs. City of Fostoria, Employer. Arbitrator Nels E. Nelson. 19 January 2019. (Appendix)

[3] Bible Gateway. Hebrews 12:1. New King James Version of The Holy Bible (NKJV). https://www.biblegateway.com/passage/?search=Hebrews+12%3A1-2&version=NKJV

[4] Federal Mediation and Conciliation Service: Arbiter Decision. Case No. 08-58518. Clayton, Moore, Grievant. March 9, 2009.

Appendix

[1] PolitiFact. "Counting up how much the NRA spends on campaigns and lobbying." Louis Jacobson. October 11, 2019. https://www.politifact.com/truth-o-meter/article/2017/oct/11/counting-up-how-much-nra-spends/

[2] Michael Bennett and Dave Zirin. *Things that Make White People Uncomfortable*. Haymarket Books. Chicago, Illinois. 2018. Print. pp. 148-152.

[3] Pew Institute. Fact Tank. Rich Morin and Andrew Mercer. "A closer look at police officers who have fired their weapon on duty." February 8, 2017. https://www.pewresearch.org/fact-tank/2017/02/08/a-closer-look-at-police-officers-who-have-fired-their-weapon-on-duty/

4 Government Technology. Ben Miller. "Just How Common Are Body Cameras in Police Departments?" June 28, 2019.
https://www.govtech.com/data/Just-How-Common-Are-Body-Cameras-in-Police-Departments.html

5 Clarke Jr., David. *Cop Under Fire: Moving Beyond Hashtags of Race, Crime & Politics for a Better America.* Worthy Publishing. Franklin, Tennessee. 2017. Print. p. 228.

RESOURCES AND RECOMMENDED READING

Big Brothers Big Sisters
Athletes for Impact (A4I)
White Rage: The Unspoken Truth of Our Racial Divide by
Carol Anderson, Ph.D.

ACKNOWLEDGEMENTS

My thanks go first to Amanda Hyde. She is the best daughter-in-law a man could ask for and the most positive person I've ever met. No matter what the situation or how dark things may be, she chooses to find the positive in everything. Amanda, thank you for being a deep listener and encouraging me to share my story with a wider audience and for jumpstarting this book project. I'm so glad you joined our family.

Micah, you jumped on board immediately and were one hundred percent supportive of this effort. You're a make-things-happen guy who helped me see that I could make this happen in my life. Thank you for being on my team.

To my wife Pam, a woman who was there with me when things got really rough and who never waivers in support. Pam, you are the love of my life. Thank you for believing in me and encouraging me to be the best man I can be.

Mommy, you started this on the day you told me that the Fostoria Police Department was hiring and that I should apply. Actually, you started this on the day I was born and have been on my side every day since. I love you so much.

Aside from my family, I owe the most thanks to my attorney Joe Hegedus. When I got fired, you were the only person I wanted on my legal team. Thank you for your keen sense of fairness, sharp legal mind, and enduring friendship.

This acknowledgement section would be incomplete if I didn't express my deep gratitude and love for my First Baptist Church family. I will be eternally grateful for your support in my darkest hour, for the BBQ fundraiser, for your laughter and songs of encouragement, and for every word that bolstered my faith.

To Cristen Iris, I felt an immediate connection the first time we talked. You understood my heart and leaned into this project by giving everything you have and encouraging me to be vulnerable and give readers everything I have. Thank you for your patience and commitment.

The first time I talked to Stephanie Chandler it was like I'd known her forever. Stephanie, I am a blessed author to have a publisher who shares my vision and is willing to partner with me to spread my message. Thank you.

Chela Hardy, you are a project manager extraordinaire. Thank you for your enthusiasm and guidance. To my cover designer, Lewis Agrell, and proofreader, George Mason, thank you both for your attention to detail and ability to reflect my intent and the spirit of my story.

Thank you to Michelle Tennant Nicholson and the Wasabi Publicity team for educating and promoting me.

And many thanks go to the Fostoria Police Department for giving me the opportunity to serve the community I grew up in and love. It was an honor.

CPSIA information can be obtained
at www.ICGtesting.com
Printed in the USA
FSHW011912010521
80904FS